Hospitality Financial Accounting

HOSPITALITY FINANCIAL ACCOUNTING

Shikha Pratap

CENTRUM PRESS
NEW DELHI-110002 (INDIA)

CENTRUM PRESS
H.O.: 4360/4, Ansari Road, Daryaganj,
New Delhi-110002 (India)
Tel: 23278000, 23261597, 23255577, 23286875
B.O.: No. 1015, Ist Main Road, BSK IIIrd Stage,
IIIrd Phase, IIIrd Block, Bengaluru-560085 (INDIA)
Tel: 080-41723429
Email: centrumpress@gmail.com
Visit us at: www.centrumpress.com

Hospitality Financial Accounting

First Edition, 2013

ISBN 978-93-81460-04-7

PRINTED IN INDIA

Printed at Balaji Offset, Delhi.

Contents

Preface

Financial Accounting is the field of accountancy concerned with the preparation of financial statements for decision makers, such as stockholders, suppliers, banks, employees, government agencies, owners, and other stakeholders. Financial capital maintenance can be measured in either nominal monetary units or units of constant purchasing power. The fundamental need for financial accounting is to reduce principal-agent problem by measuring and monitoring agents' performance and reporting the results to interested users. Financial accountancy is used to prepare accounting information for people outside the organization or not involved in the day-to-day running of the company. Management accounting provides accounting information to help managers make decisions to manage the business. In short, Financial Accounting is the process of summarizing financial data taken from an organization's accounting records and publishing in the form of annual (or more frequent) reports for the benefit of people outside the organization. Financial accountancy is governed by both local and international accounting standards. Financial accountants produce financial statements based on Generally Accepted Accounting Principles of a respective country. In particular cases financial statements must be prepared according to the International Financial Reporting Standards. Consistent with other roles in today's corporation, management accountants have a dual reporting relationship. As a strategic partner and provider of decision based financial and operational information, management accountants are responsible for managing the business team and at the same time having to report relationships and responsibilities to the corporation's finance organization.

The activities management accountants provide inclusive of forecasting and planning, performing variance analysis, reviewing and monitoring costs inherent in the business are ones that have dual accountability to both finance and the business team. Examples of tasks where accountability may be more meaningful to the business management team vs. the corporate finance department are the development of new product costing, operations research, business driver metrics, sales management scorecarding, and client profitability analysis. See Financial modeling. Conversely, the preparation of certain financial reports, reconciliations of the financial data to source systems, risk and regulatory reporting will be more useful to the corporate finance team as they are charged with aggregating certain financial information from all segments of the corporation.

In corporations that derive much of their profits from the information economy, such as banks, publishing houses, telecommunications companies and defence contractors, IT costs are a significant source of uncontrollable spending, which in size is often the greatest corporate cost after total compensation costs and property related costs.

The book introduces the fundamentals of financial accounting through examples from hotels, restaurants, and clubs. Even managers who feel they are not "numbers people" will easily understand the accounting process and its function in hospitality operations. This means understanding fundamental accounting concepts, developing solid financial analysis abilities, and then applying them to understand and improve the operational performance of their hotel or restaurant.

—*Author*

1

Introduction

In general, hotels offer two major types of services: (a) accommodation and (b) dining services. Based on the quality and extent of services provided, location, bedroom, front office/ reception, food and beverage, general facilities (service and staff), and special facilities (i.e., business centre, limousine services and airport transfers), hotels are further classified as Deluxe, First Class, Standard, and Economy.

Hotel guests can expect a room with private bath, telephone, radio, and television, in addition to such customer services such as laundry, valet, cleaning and pressing. Aside from the services mentioned, hotels have other facilities: function rooms, ballrooms, health spas, coffee shops, dining rooms, cocktail lounges or night clubs, gift shops or newsstand-tobacco counters, and business centres for social occasions, health buffs, and business conferences.

Customers of the industry include the domestic household, foreign visitors and institutional buyers. Research shows that the domestic household's selection of hotels and other lodging facilities are affected mainly by three factors:

1) competitive pricing;
2) availability of services and facilities for children; and
3) type and extent of free services (i.e., free local calls, continental breakfast, etc.).

Meanwhile, notwithstanding the currency and economic turmoil in Asia, the Philippine tourism industry posted a 2.17

billion arrivals in 1999. In the past five years, visitor arrivals have been growing at an annual average of 9%, contributing more than US$2.3 billion per year to the country's foreign exchange earnings. Hotels are the most popular source of accommodation for more than 50% of foreign visitors. Indeed, more than 40% of a foreign visitor's average daily expenditure is accounted for by accommodations. While food and beverage consumption for about 23%.

Institutional buyers often patronize the restaurant services offered by the hotel sub-sector in promoting their products, training their employees, and holding company gatherings. The wholesale and retail (19.6%), nonferrous smelting and refining plants (18%), public administration and defence (17.4%), and finance (11.6%) industries are among the hotel subsector's biggest clients, accounting for more than 66% of the latter's total output.

In response to the growing demand for hotel accommodations, the last five years witnessed the steady expansion of every segment of the hotel industry. On the average, the total number of hotel rooms has grown from 11,742 in 1995 to 13,090 in 1999, an average of 2.3%. Standard hotels experienced the largest growth at an annual average of 17.1%, from 1,671 rooms in 1995 to 3,100 in 1999. Followed by first class hotels, with an average of 9.6% annually, from 1,798 rooms in 1995 to 2,559 rooms in 1999.

Hotel entry barriers, which include economies of scale, infrastructure, and product differentiation, are significant particularly for those who will venture in deluxe or first class operations.

Economies of scale force a new entrant to come in at relatively large scale and risk strong reaction from existing firms. Consequently, requiring substantial start-up costs. As only a small percentage of the country's potential business and tourist areas have developed communication, sewerage and disposal systems, and roads and, the lack of infrastructure is likewise an industry entry barrier. Finally, product differentiation exists in the industry. Established firms have brand identification and customer loyalties, which stem from past advertising and customer service.

Despite relatively high barriers to entry, however, the number of hotels has increased by more than 11% percent in the last five years. Optimism about the domestic economy, the lack of viable accommodations alternative, abundance of competent potential hotel workers and professionals, and the relative ease in procuring required inputs encourage entry into the industry. Opportunities for hoteliers also arise from the country's strategic location. The Philippines is situated in the centre of Asia, home of the fastest-growing economies in the world. Moreover, government, industry association and trade union cooperation provides the industry with a strong support system.

While there are already quite a number of players in the market, the hotel industry can be characterized by still a rigid competitive structure. Product differentiation prevents any hotel from monopolizing the market.

According to the Top 7000 Corporations, the fifty-two (52) top hotels and other lodging facilities posted a modest increase of 7% in combined gross revenue from PHP12.4 billion in 1998 to PHP13.2 billion in 1999. Combined net income in for top hotels and other lodging facilities, likewise, went up 19.2% during the same period, from PHP709 million in 1998 to PHP845 million the following year. Profitability also increased, 9.1%, from 0.044 in 1998 to 0.048 in 1999.

The top ten hotels accounted for 61.4% of the sub-sector's gross revenue in 1999. Among the three hotels and other lodging facilities with the highest 1999 gross revenues are Edsa Shangri-la Hotel and Resort, Inc., PHP1.3 billion (9.7% revenue share), Manila Peninsula, PHP1.1 billion (8.1% revenue share) and New World International Development Philippines, PHP983 million (7.4% revenue share).

Based on occupancy rates, however, the Mandarin Oriental, the Makati Shangrila and the Manila Diamond Hotel topped the DOT accredited de luxe hotels category for the period January to April 2000 with occupancy rates of 81.5%, 77.1% and 77.1%, respectively. Traders Hotel, Holiday Inn Manila, and Manila Midtown Hotel, on the other hand, led the seven DOT accredited first class hotels during the same period with occupancy rates of

67.75%, 66.27%, and 66.25%, respectively. Among the 40 DOT accredited standard hotels, the Sulo Hotel, the Century Imperial Suites, and the City States Tower Hotel registered the highest occupancy rates at 74.71%, 69.54%, and 68%, respectively. Finally, among the fifteen DOT accredited economy hotels occupancy rates ranged from 76-20% from January to April 2000 with Jade Vine Executive Inn, El Cielito Tourist Inn, and Swagman Hotel leading at 76.02%, 52.22%, and 51.75%, respectively.

In general, the hotel sub-sector's strength lies in the following: the ability to innovate, a pool of competent potential workers/ professionals, and technology development. Pressure on hotel prices, on the other hand, comes from the drive "for value for money".

Increased operating efficiency obtained through the computerization has helped to reduce costly waste in the supply chain. However, higher labour, raw materials, and utility costs continue to push operating costs up. Finally, in the macro level, economic and political factors affect the performance of the tourism industry. In the past two years, for example, declining disposable income resulting from the Asian currency crisis and political instability resulted in a 3% contraction in tourist arrivals in 1998 and a 1% increase in 1999.

Restaurants

Participants in the restaurant sub-sector provide food and drinks, be it selfservice or full-service. The sub-sector caters to both household and institutional buyers. The Philippine household market is segmented into five income groups (A, B, C, D and E). Based on the preliminary results of the 1997 Family Income and Expenditure Survey (FIES), the middle income bracket has expanded from the 1994 level from 28% of the total number of families in the economy to 30%.

The FIES data indicate that families have experienced improvements in their income in 1997 from 1994, which indicates an increase in the local population's buying power. Furthermore, FIES data show that spending on food consumed outside the home has been increasing from 3.1%in 1985 to 4.7% in 1997. With total family expenditures increasing more than four times during the period, this translated to more than PHP66.8 billion spent on restaurant services in 1997. Research bore out that top five quality characteristics that influence the Filipinos choice of restaurants and fastfood outlets, ranked according to importance, are flavor and taste, value for money/nutrient content, presentation and packaging, variety, and systematic ordering and selling.

Meanwhile, institutional buyers employ the services of the restaurant industry for occasions such as seminars, workshops, meetings, company celebrations, and marketing and promotional activities. Among the hotel and restaurant industry's main institutional markets are the wholesale and retail trade (30.4%), air transport (23%), and the other recreational and cultural services sectors (5.7%).

To date, there are about 45,220 restaurant establishments in the domestic economy catering to the dining requirements of a constantly expanding market. An estimated 80%, or more than 36,000, of these establishments are classified under the fast food sub-sector.

Low barriers to entry characterize the industry. Capital investments particularly for franchises can range anywhere from PHP500,000 to PHP10,000,000. Training, marketing and distribution channels are arranged by the franchisor. Likewise, as the franchisor provides the new entrant fully developed management and production systems, prior knowledge and experience are not required of franchisees. These characteristics of franchising, particularly of food establishments, make the business very attractive for new entrepreneurs.

The proliferation of one-stop shopping malls that offer various recreational facilities and amenities, likewise, eases the entry of potential restaurant and fast food players. These malls spare the restaurant industry from spending extensive business development studies for their outlets; mall magnates Henry Sy and John Gokongwei Jr. have established formidable track records in building malls. The industry in which the restaurant and fast food firms operate has increasing consumer demand for every improving product. The growth is proven by the rapid expansion of food outlets in key areas in Metro Manila and the provinces. The popularity of fast food establishments came in the 1980's, and over the last years, the industry has consistently posted double-digit growth rates.

Competition is fierce in the restaurant industry, particularly the fast food sub-sector. The market is large but consumers are price conscious and exhibit brand loyalty. With a wide range of restaurants and fast food establishments to choose from, pricing schemes and marketing strategies determine market shares. Market strategies of industry players, therefore, aim to achieve two primary objectives: 1) hammer in "value-for-money" concepts; and 2) create brand consciousness and loyalty.

Market shares in the restaurants are won or lost in pricing. Industry players offer regularly offer price cuts and discounts to lure in new customers. Moreover, major players invest heavily in advertising to create brand consciousness and loyalty. Marketing strategies include raffle draws, free gift items and specially prized meal combinations, discounted toys and school items for every certain minimum food purchase. Celebrity endorsements are used in the hopes that the market will identify with the endorser.

Likewise, intense competition urges players to come up with new products to capture bigger market shares. Restauranteurs have to be keen at finding the latest food and wine concoctions here and abroad and adapting them to local taste. Targeting the Filipino's tastebuds, several fastfood chains that usually serve only western food have introduced items that appeal to the local market's palate.

Raising quality standards and improving service have also been focal points of competition, particularly in the fast food sub-sector. Players give incentives and compensations to motivate employees to be efficient on their jobs and thus help maintain the fast food outlet's high standards of quality service and cleanliness. Also, a major importance in a fast food and restaurant is courteous and friendly personnel. Not surprisingly, a speedy service is among the more salient attributes people would highly expect from a fast food/restaurant.

Finally, to keep their share of the market, food chains find it necessary to extend their service coverage by setting up other branches. Industry players who have outlets that are visible in Metro Manila and in other key urban cities are ones who are most likely to take in more profits. Malls, university areas, and other places where there is heavy pedestrian traffic are the usual places where fast food and restaurants are highly patronized.

Restaurant and fast food industry players balance their marketing concerns with the rising operation costs particularly that of imported food ingredients. Profit margin erosion is usually remedied by either increasing prices of final product/service or cut corners in production or the delivery of service. Either solution may result in a shrinking customer base.

Thus, no one restaurant or fastfood chain completely dominate the subsector. In 1999, the 278 top restaurants in the Philippines posted a total of PHP33.7 billion in gross revenues, 8.6% higher than the 1998 PHP31 billion. Net income for the same firms climbed slightly from PHP811.9 million in 1998 to PHP815 million. Asset and equity investment in likewise increased during the period by 24.3% and 23%, respectively.

Profitability for the top 278 firms, however, fell 16% from 1998's 0.12 to 1999's 0.10 as the industry required more capital, 0.63 unit in 1999 from 0.55 in 1998, to produce one extra unit of output.

In the fast food segment, Jollibee remains at the top with an estimated 29.4% share of the restaurant sub-sector's gross revenue in 1999 and about 50% market share of the local hamburger-segment patrons.

Meanwhile, the local fine dining and speciality restaurants segment accounted for less than 20% of the restaurant sub-sector's 1999 gross revenue. Although top ten restaurant chains account for more than 50% of the local fine dining segment market, the biggest player Perf Restaurants, Inc. ranked 9th, with a 1.6% of the total restaurant sub-sector's gross revenue.

In general, the restaurant industry's strength lies primarily in technology development. Technology transfer, franchising, allows interested parties to operate a franchise without prior experience or training. Domestic and international food chains and franchises facilitate transfer of technology in the local restaurant sub-sector. They provide training of potential employees and employ strict quality control systems. Raw materials are likewise provided by the franchisor.

Finally, there is no real threat of external substitutes to the services provided by the restaurant industry. Indeed, it is competition between the subsectors of the industry that determines market share.

Laws Hindering/Facilitating

Laws that hinder or facilitate the hotel and restaurant industry include Executive Order 219, which established the domestic and international civil aviation liberalization policy, the Investment Priorities Plan (IPP) 2000, Intellectual Property Rights, and the Labour Code provisions on the employment of foreign nationals.

Provisions of EO 219 opened the domestic airline industry market to competition, which resulted in the expansion of airline seat capacity, reduced airfare and the elimination of the so-called "missionary routes". Combined, EO 219 led to a significant increase in tourism, thus expanding on of the hotel and restaurant industry's main market.

The IPP 2000 offers fiscal incentives to investors in, among others, the tourism industry (i.e., tourist accommodation facilities, which refer to hotel, apartelle, tourist inns, pension house, and resorts, tourism estates, tourist buses, and restoration of historical and cultural sites/properties).

All franchise agreements with foreign franchisors are registered with Intellectual Property Rights office as well as licensing, technical assistance and services, technology transfer and distribution agreements.

Foreign franchisors in the Philippines, similar to other industries, are subject to the restrictions on ownership, 40%. The laws on technology transfer, however, guarantee franchisors in the Philippines royalties of 5% and a maximum allowable term of technology transfer arrangements of ten years. Finally, foreign national employment in the hotel and restaurant industry is subject to the tripartite agreement signed in 1992 by the Department of Tourism, Department of Labour and Employment and the Bureau of Immigration. The agreement addresses the following issues regarding the employment of foreign nationals in the hotel and restaurant industry: positions open to foreign nationals, procedures in the issuance of visa/permits, and disciplinary/penal provisions.

Foreign Market Demand

Franchising allows local hotel and restaurant establishments to enter foreign markets. Transfer of technology, franchising, however, is subject to the unique laws of the market the hotel and restaurant firms intend to penetrate.

These laws, which are as varied as the countries that implement them, commonly address issues such as royalties, repatriation of profits, employment of foreign nationals, property ownership, taxes, and the like. International deployment of hotel and restaurant workers and professionals, on the other hand, are subject to laws pertaining to the practice of their profession. Indeed, most countries have policies preventing foreign professionals from practicing their profession in the domestic market. In the last five years, hotel and restaurant related workers and professional deployment averaged more than six thousand seven hundred forty per year. An estimated 75% of all hotel and restaurant professionals deployed during the period were cooks, waiters, bartenders and other related workers.

Filipino hotel and restaurant workers and professionals are known for their competence, trainability, and ease in adapting to different environments and are, therefore, in demand in the international market. Most hotel and restaurant related workers and professionals during the five-year period were deployed to United Arab Emirates, Saudi Arabia, Kuwait, Papua New Guinea, Singapore Malaysia, and the United States.

Industry Training Needs

A primary source of hotel and restaurant professionals' training are the various schools and universities that offer courses in hotel and restaurant management. A pioneer, in this area is the Asian Institute of Tourism, which established in 1976.

Besides providing high quality education and training to students who will be the industry's future managers, entrepreneurs and technical experts, the Institute also conducts research as well as offer professional and technical programs training for the hospitality industry

AIT's lead was followed by other educational institutions. Examples of schools offering such formal education include De La Salle University (Dasmarinas and the College of St. Benilde), the University of the Philippines, and University of Santo Tomas, and the Hotel and Tourism Institute of the Philippines Foundation, Inc., to name a few. Such courses involve basic aspects of hotel operations including the front office, food and beverage, house keeping, and room service, culinary skills, customer care, marketing, accounting, as well as European language skills.

Aside from the formal training potential hotel and restaurant workers and professionals receive from the academe, hotel establishments conduct on-the-job training, apprenticeship, management training, and career development seminars.

A selected few are deployed to training schools managed by the hotels themselves (i.e., Dusit). Technical Education Skills Development Authority (TESDA) also offers training and certification for certain hotel and restaurant industry entry-level positions.

Despite progress made in training hotel and restaurant workers and professionals, resulting in quality personnel, as a continuously evolving industry, a more intensive management training that combine theoretical as well as practical exposure to planning, organizing, staffing, communication, and coping in organizations. Moreover, training programs that strengthen technical skills particularly computer operations, especially with the increasing utilization of information technology in the industry (i.e., reservations, accounting systems, and point-of-sale-system for restaurants) would complement latest "software and hardware" employment.

Recommendations

The following recommendations are presented in the context of the country's commitment to enhance the competitiveness of the hotel and restaurant industry.

The intent is to enable the sector to compete more effectively in the local and domestic markets and to enhance the marketability of the country's hotel and restaurant industry's manpower in the international market.

The determinants of a subsector's competitiveness would depend on: 1) the level of expertise/competence of local professionals/businesses, 2) the degree of openness of foreign markets and their demand for local expertise, and 3) the degree of openness of the local regulatory framework (i.e. absence or presence of reciprocity provisions).

Among the recommendations to enhance the hotel and restaurant industry's competitiveness include, but are not limited to, the promotion of sustainable tourism, improvement of the legal/regulatory environment (particularly those that pertain to the GATS Philippines commitments), offering systems incentives to promote investment into the hotel and restaurant industry, human resource development (i.e., training and continuing education), and strengthening industry linkages.

In the area of sustainable development, it is recommended that programs should incorporate the following principles:

1. Natural sites should be protected and strict provisions added to prevent pollution and to control the use of energy and natural resources;
2. Existing cultural practices in such areas which are helpful to safeguarding the sites should be upheld;

Eco-tourism should be promoted.

1. Extension of subsidies and loans for the development of tourist facilities.
2. Diversification of transportation, destinations and types of tourism for balanced tourism development. Said policies would promote tourism and its allied industries, including

the hotel and restaurant industry, by expanding their primary market, domestic and international tourists.

Recognizing the contributions of foreign professionals in the hotel and restaurant industry, legal/regulatory environment recommendations include, among other things, the liberalization of foreign nationals' practice of their profession in the country. The review of the country's bilateral agreements on reciprocal recognition of professionals that may have inconsistencies with the general obligations of GATS is likewise recommended so as to benefit the thousands of hotel and restaurant professionals who are deployed abroad annually.

Systems incentives recommendations, including the granting of tax exemptions for renovations, are designed to attract more investments into the sector as well as to lower the costs for existing players.

In order to enhance the sector's inherent comparative advantage in human resources, it is recommended that the capability of educational institutions be strengthened to satisfy industry's need for professionals, particularly in areas where there is a lack of supply. This includes the strengthening of the basic education system to enable elementary & secondary schools to equip students the basic skills, primarily the 4Rs (reading, writing, arithmetic, and right conduct); the promotion of continuing education to enhance the skills of professionals and technical workers to make them more competitive abroad and less vulnerable to displacement by foreigners who enter the local market.

More important is to encourage the training and certification (i.e., from the Technical Education and Skills Development Agency) of basic entry-level positions in the hotel and restaurant industry.

Developing industry network and linkages is likewise included in the recommendation. Developing and strengthening linkage among industry players will assure industry players a stronger voice when dealing with government regarding the formulation of national policies concerning their respective industries. This will also open up opportunities in terms of pooling of resources, exchange of information, and the conduct of training for members. Industry associations should also take an active role in the process of negotiating mutual recognition agreements (MRAs) because they are the one who are most familiar with their members' needs, capabilities, and preparedness to face liberalization.

Developing and strengthening linkage between industry and academe could be done through on-the-job training (OJT) or apprenticeship agreements that would enhance the skills of college students through hands-on training and exposure to the actual workplace.

The parties could also come up with consultancy arrangements that would enable firms to benefit from the research capabilities of the faculty of schools, and that would enable academe to tap the expertise of professionals in their academic programs. Finally, industry and academe could institutionalize systems for the continuing education of company personnel either through graduate studies or through in-house training/customized programs that could be provided by schools to the firms.

Developing linkages between industry and intermediate industries (i.e., booking and travel agents) can expand the industry's market. Travel agents and meeting planners, for example, can and do influence a substantial number of bookings. Building these relationship with intermediaries begin with giving the them access to more precise information on the hotel's brand promises to ensure a correct and satisfactory transaction, as well as providing promotions and incentives and making timely commission payments.

Meanwhile, in the area of financing, banks should be encourage to create special financing schemes to help small-and medium-scale hotel and restaurant firms gain access to more capital needed for investment in advanced technology, and to help them bridge working capital requirements; to provide funds for training and development of local manpower, particularly for small-and mediumscale firms; and to simplify requirements for availing of loans to encourage firms, particularly the smaller players, to take advantage of financing schemes. In terms of the application of information technology in the hotel and restaurant industry, players can explore the following options:

1) adopt: onscreen informational and promotional guide listing the hotel's outlets and services, through the in-room television hotel guests may view their folios, receive messages, book reservations at hotel restaurants, participate in guest satisfaction surveys, and conduct express checkouts;
2) use in hotel and restaurant marketing, advertising and promotion via the internet (i.e., websites);
3) access market trends (i.e., tourism, culinary, business services, etc.) on the web;
4) use in training (i.e., computer-based training); and
5) use in waste management systems.

Depending on the perspective, monitoring the hotel and restaurant industry's performance can be done by several institutions. Designated government agencies, for example, set policies and guidelines pertaining to customer physical safety and satisfaction (i.e., in terms of accommodations and health and sanitary standards). They also guard against fraud and, ideally, promote truth in advertising and transparency in product information (i.e., the Department of Trade and Industry approves all types of marketing schemes pertaining to promotions such as raffles, price discounts, etc.). Moreover, public institutions also monitor entry and exit of players in the industry and specific performance indicators (i.e., measured occupancy rates, financial highlights, deployment of workers and professionals, etc.).

Meanwhile, industry associations, the Hotel and Restaurant Association of the Philippines in particular, take on the role of undertaking programs and projects that will upgrade and professionalize the industry, promoting unity and mutual cooperation among industry members, encouraging and fostering high ethical standards, and representing the sector's interest matters of government regulatory policies/laws/rules affecting the industry.

Finally, trade unions safeguard the rights and welfare of industry workers and professionals. They work closely with government and industry participants in improving working conditions and employee performance (i.e., recommending additional training and or certification) and in defending employee rights. The tourism industry is a major contributor to the world economy. According to the estimates of the World Tourism Organization (WTO), international tourism alone generated $1.4 trillion in receipts (4.1 percent of World GDP) in 2000. Estimates of the World Travel and Tourism Council (WTTC), on the other hand, put the impact of tourism on the economy at a much higher level because it includes domestic tourism. As reported by the WTTC, tourism grossed US$566 billion in world visitor exports and created employment for 73.1 million persons in the year 2000.

The Caribbean is the most tourism-oriented region in the world. It is estimated that in 2000, tourism employed 3.1 million people either directly or indirectly, thus accounting for 13.4 percent of total employment. Direct employment in the tourism characteristic industries alone amounted to 5 percent of total employment. Visitor expenditures contributed an estimated US$17 billion, or 18.4 percent, to export revenues. Countries whose international tourism receipts exceeded 5 percent of GDP or 10 percent of export revenues are considered to be "tourism countries" for the purposes of the World Trade Organization. Tourism-related portions of GDP estimated by the WTTC for a number of countries are shown in Annex J. Annex K, on the other hand, shows international receipts be region.

Indeed, global travel is expected to grow rapidly for at least the next 20 years. Worldwide arrivals were expected to expand from 613 million in 1997 to an estimated 700 million in 2000, 1 billion by 2010 and 1.6 billion by 2020. Improving balance of trade means more business for European tourist destinations. Europe will remain the strongest magnet for tourism, with arrivals growth holding between 3% and 4%.

Extreme strength of the US economy is expected to stimulate demand for tourism and hospitality services among American business and vacation travellers.

Low Asian currency values will continue to promote travel to the Far East, for so long as they last.

The Philippines, according to the WTTC, is positioned at the epicenter of global travel and tourism growth and development. In 1997, tourism contributed 8.7% of the country's GDP, generating 2.3 million jobs (or one in every nine nationwide), and accounting for some 10.5% of Philippine investments. The trade surplus from tourism for the same period was estimated at PHP22 billion, driven mainly by visitor spending. The WTTC expects tourism to contribute 10.9% of the country's GDP by 2007, and to generate as much as 1.4 million more jobs between 1998 and 2007.

According to the Department of Tourism, international arrivals in 1999 stood at 2.17 million, a slight increase from the previous year's total of 2.15 million visitors. Despite the economic crisis suffered by its Asian markets, the Philippines' foreign exchange receipts from tourism went up by 5.83% from $2.41 billion in 1998 to $2.55 billion in 1999.

Moreover, the Philippines enjoyed the highest repeat visitors in Asia at 54.22 percent, indicating that the tourism sector can survive external threats and competition in the region. In terms of market share, the USA continued to supply the biggest volume of arrivals at 21.36 percent, followed by Japan and Hong Kong, which accounted for 17.85 percent and 7.38 percent of the total traffic, respectively. Other high yielding markets include Taiwan (6.62%), Korea (6.13%), UK (4.1%), Australia (3.58%), and Canada (2.99%).

As tourism serves as the main market for hotel and restaurant services, increase in visitor traffic over the past ten years resulted in a corresponding boom in the hotel and restaurant industry. During the last decade, the hotel and restaurant industry has flourished even as it struggled to cope with difficult challenges. New hotels mushroomed in the capital while older hotels did their best to spruce-up both their interiors and upgrade services. Likewise, the growth of the restaurant sub-sector, the number of players and the variety of services offered had been notable during the same period.

This is just a taste of years to come. Indeed, as the global population continues to grow and change, science and technology will tighten their hold on business and society, and the world will knit itself ever more tightly into a single market. As foreign visitors depend primarily on the hotel and restaurant industry for their accommodation and dining needs, growing world tourism will offer both opportunities and trials will abound for the world's hotel and restaurant industry. It is in this context that this paper presents information meant to:

1. define the coverage and structure of the hotel and restaurant industry
2. identify the industry's forward linkages (market)
3. identify the hotel and restaurant industry's backward linkages (suppliers)
4. identify the laws affecting the trade in hotel and restaurant services
5. determine the industry's market potential/foreign market demand
6. determine the industry's supply capability
7. identify the sector's training needs
8. identify the industry's strengths, weaknesses, opportunities and threats
9. recommend policies that will enhance the industry's competitiveness.

The Industry

The hotel and restaurant industry is the combination of institutions, supporting human resources, financing mechanisms, information systems, organizational structures that link institutions and resources that cater to the needs of domestic and foreign travellers.

Institutions include government departments and agencies, private providers of lodging and catering services, such as hotels, motels, restaurants, fast food establishments, educational institutions that provide training, and other types of organizations responsible for the promotion of hospitality services. The local hotel industry is already in its mature stage characterized by overcapacity of available rooms and gradual standardization of prizes across categories of services.

The members of local restaurant and fast food industry, on the other hand, is in its growth stage and has increasing consumer demand for every improving product. The growth is proven by the rapid expansion of food outlets in key areas in Metro Manila and the provinces. The popularity of fast food establishments came in the 1980's, and over the last years, the industry has consistently posted double-digit growth rates.

Supporting human resources include hotel and restaurant managers and assistant managers, housekeeping supervisors, security personnel, chefs, cooks, wâiters, bartenders, and other related workers and professionals directly involved in hotel and restaurant services. Financing mechanisms include equity infusions of local and foreign investors, particularly for international hotel chains and loans from fiduciary institutions.

Information systems include computer networks within and among institutions including electronic mail, printed media such as journals, magazines, and newsletters, telephone systems including voice mail and data transmission, interactive multimedia, and other information media technology that facilitates sharing or exchange of information, summarizes and collates data. Linking organizational mechanisms are industry associations and trade unions that facilitate communication among organizational units including government agencies.

Definition

The hotel and rest^urant industry definition used in this study follows the Philippine Standard Industrial Classification. The industry is disaggregated into two sub-sectors: hotel and restaurant.

The hotel sub-sector includes the various lodging units of different sizes and standards located both in urban and rural communities. The restaurant sub-sector, on the other hand, includes places that serve food and drinks, be it self-service or full-service. This covers a range of services including fine dining speciality restaurants, fast food outlets, canteens, and food courts. Fine dining and speciality restaurants offer a wide variety of international cuisines. Meanwhile, so-called fast food restaurants usually operate in chains or as franchises, are heavily advertised, and offer limited menus-typically comprising of hamburgers, hotdogs, fried chicken, or pizza and their complements – likewise originated in the United States. Fast foods have the advantage of speed, convenience, and familiarity to diners who may eat in the restaurant or take their food home. In the Philippines, about 80% of the establishments in restaurant industry belong to the fast food sub-sector.

Contribution to the Economy

The hotel and restaurant industry's contribution to the Philippine economy grew from 1.29% to the 1994 gross domestic product (GDP) to 1.35% in 1998, a 4.6% increase. In terms of the gross national product, the sector's contribution went up slightly, 1.6%, from 1.26% in 1994 to 1.28% in 1998. The hotel and restaurant industry continued to employ about 1% of the country's labour force.

Structure

In 1994, according to the National Statistics Office (NSO), there were 46,930 firms belonging to the hotel and restaurant industry, employing a total of 221,954 people. At the time, each peso investment in labour contributed PHP4.40 to the industry's total output while each peso investment in capital yielded a PHP1.27 contribution to the same.

As a component of the services sector, the hotel and restaurant industry accounted for 37.4% of the establishments, 46.2% of employment, and 43.6% of gross revenue of the Philippine services sector. The restaurant sub-sector dominated the industry, accounting for more than 95% of the establishments, employment, and gross revenue of the sector.

In terms of regional distribution, the National Capital Region (NCR) Southern Tagalog, and Southern Mindanao regions, combined, account for the greatest number of hotel and restaurant establishments, 45.9%. The three, likewise, employ 51.7% of workers in the hotel and restaurant industry. Finally, NCR, region IV and region XI generate 52.7% of the sector's gross revenue.

In particular, Department of Tourism statistics show that deluxe hotels are concentrated in Manila. Being the main entry point for foreign travellers, the capital is an attractive location for hoteliers. In secondary destinations, only Cebu has deluxe hotels such as Shangri-la Mactan and Plantation Bay (with a total of 359 rooms). However, Cebu is also fast catching up with Metro Manila with the entry of Waterfront, and Mariott Hotel. In other provinces, standard and economy hotels proliferate in cities and tourist destinations.

Most fastfood establishments are, likewise, located in the National Capital Region and in key cities of regions in Central Luzon and Southern Tagalog. Emerging urban centres outside Luzon, such as Metro Cebu and Metro Davao are becoming the target locations of outlet expansion by major players as well. Meanwhile, the average occupancy rates of DOT accredited hotels fluctuated annually from 62% in 1995 to 59% in 1999. The highest posted occupancy rate was that of 1997's at 70%. By classification, deluxe hotels fared well, consistently posting the highest occupancy rates among the four hotel categories, an average of 68.3% over the five-year period. First class hotels were at a distant second at 58.9%. Occupancy rates of standard and economy hotels during the same period averaged 58.8% and 48%, respectively.

In terms of length of stay, however, guests stay longer in standard hotels than in the higher-rated establishments. Standard hotel guests stay an average of 3.03 nights compared to the 2.66 nights and 2.13 nights average stay in deluxe and first class hotels, respectively.

Hotel entry barriers, which include economies of scale, infrastructure, and product differentiation, are significant particularly for those who will venture in deluxe or first class operations.

Economies of scale force a new entrant to come in at relatively large scale and risk strong reaction from existing firms. Consequently, requiring substantial start-up costs. To date, with the appreciation of land and high construction costs, this could range from PHP1.2 billion to PHP3 billion, depending on the number of rooms and floors and amenities. Even just to build apartelles and standard hotel would require investments of about PHP25 million to PHP55 million. Moreover, an entrant would need high start-up costs from advertising, image building to offset leverage of existing prominent hotels. Training and development costs, necessary for quality hospitality services, are also considerable.

Infrastructure is also another barrier to entry in the case of the Philippines. Communication systems, sewerage and disposal systems, roads and highways are vital to the business. Presently, only a small percentage of the country's potential business and tourist areas has been developed.

Finally, product differentiation exists in the industry. Established firms have brand identification and customer loyalties, which stem from past advertising and customer service.

Hotel chains constitute a classic application of brand strategy. Brands are a quick way for hotels and hotel chains to identify and differentiate themselves in the minds of the customers. A brand symbolizes the essence of the customer's perceptions of hotel chains, its products, and services. The favourable or unfavorable attitudes and perceptions formed by brand influence a customer's hotel preference. Despite relatively high barriers to entry, however, there are 76 hotels with 13,320 rooms in Metro Manila alone. Deluxe hotels number 16 (6,767 rooms); first class hotels, 8 (2,577 rooms); standard hotels, 33 (2,947 rooms); and 19 economy hotels (1,024 rooms). The number of rooms increased by more than 11% percent in the last five years. Optimism about the domestic economy, the lack of viable accommodations alternative, abundance of competent potential hotel workers and professionals, and the relative ease in procuring required inputs encourage entry into the industry.

Opportunities for hoteliers also arise from the country's strategic location. The Philippines is situated in the centre of Asia, home of the fastest-growing economies in the world. The archipelago lies southeast of Hong Kong, northeast of Singapore and almost directly north of Kota Kinabalu in Malaysia and Bali,

Indonesia. Owing to its accessibility and strategic location, the Philippines is a natural mecca of commerce.

Moreover, government, industry association and trade union cooperation provides the industry with a strong support system. The Philippine government actively promotes the country through its numerous tourism programs. It actively lobbies for the opportunity to host international events. The Miss Universe Pageant and World Expo, for instance, encourage tourists to visit the Philippine Islands.

Government effort is complemented by the strong support of industry associations and trade unions (i.e., Hotel and Restaurant Association of the Philippines and the National Union of Workers in the Hotel Restaurant & Allied Industries), which enable the hotel industry, among other things, to undertake programs and projects that upgrade and professionalize the sector and to influence government regulatory policies/laws/rules affecting the industry. Indeed, Manila has plenty of first class hotels. Many like the Westin Philippine Plaza and Century Park Sheraton offer reductions of 40% in the low season from June to September. Others, like the Manila Midtown Hotel, may cut their price by 50% for a stay of four weeks. The elegant Manila Hotel can be ranked with the Raffles in Singapore, Oriental in Bangkok and Peninsula in Hong Kong as among the oldest and most reputable hotels in Southeast Asia.

While there are already quite a number of players in the market, the hotel industry can be characterized by still a rigid competitive structure. Hotels sell more or less the same service but differ in quality and style. The better and wider the service, the higher the rates.

No single hotel, however, monopolizes the market or has power over the rates of rooms or of other services that are offered. Further differentiation is reflected on the variety of restaurants and coffee shops that they have and on other amenities that they offer – each catering to a specific need of clients. According to the Top 7000 Corporations and the Next 5000 Corporations, the fifty-two (52) top hotels and other lodging facilities posted an increase of more than 7% in combined gross revenue from PHP12.4 billion in 1998 to PHP13.2 billion in 1999. Combined net income for top hotels and other lodging facilities, likewise, went up during the same period, from PHP709 million in 1998 to PHP845 million the following year. Profitability also rose by more than 12%, from 0.057 in 1998 to 0.064 in 1999. The top ten hotels accounted for 61.8% of the sub-sector's gross revenue in 1999. Among the three hotels and other lodging facilities with the highest 1999 gross revenues are Edsa Shangri-la Hotel and Resort, Inc., PHP1.9 billion (9.7% revenue share), Manila Peninsula, PHP1.07 billion (8% revenue share) and New World International Development Philippines PHP983 million (7% revenue share).

Based on occupancy rates, the Mandarin Oriental, the Makati Shangrila and the Manila Diamond Hotel topped the DOT accredited de luxe hotels category for the period January to April 2000 with occupancy rates of 81.5%, 77.1% and 77.1%, respectively. Traders Hotel, Holiday Inn Manila, and Manila Midtown Hotel, on the other hand, led the seven DOT accredited first class hotels during the same period with occupancy rates of 67.75%, 66.27%, and 66.25%, respectively. Among the 40 DOT accredited standard hotels, the Sulo Hotel, the Century Imperial Suites, and the City States Tower Hotel registered the highest occupancy rates at 74.71%, 69.54%, and 68%, respectively. Finally, among the 15 DOT accredited economy hotels occupancy rates ranged from 76-20% from January to April 2000 with Jade Vine Executive Inn, El Cielito Tourist Inn, and Swagman Hotel leading at 76.02%, 52.22%, and 51.75%, respectively.

In general, the hotel sub-sector's strength lies in the following: the ability to innovate, a pool of competent potential workers/professionals, and technology development. Developing services to better meet the needs of its clients allows hoteliers to maintain, if not expand, its market. Anticipating the potential requirements of a travelling businessman, for example, makes a hotel more attractive. Hotel Intercon capitalized on its ideal location and deliberately put in place amenities and facilities to suit the changing needs of the business traveler. Some of these eventually became the standard followed by other hotels here and abroad.

Pan Pacific Hotel, on the other hand, decided to revive the "butler" tradition. Every guest is provided with a butler who can be counted upon to do and anticipate a guests bidding.

Filipinos are among the best-educated and most easily trainable people in Asia. They are capable of performing even the most complicated task with world-class competence.

Filipino hotel employees are reputed to possess the following characteristics, which give local hotels an advantage over their regional competitors: they are resourceful, easy to train, and can speak English. Friendly by nature, Filipinos have a special way of making strangers feel welcome. Hospitality in the Philippines is both a tradition and an art. Moreover, among Asians, Filipinos are the most fluent in written and spoken English. Since English is the world's universal business language, tourists and business travellers alike are always pleasantly surprised at the absence of any language barrier in their dealings with Filipino hotel and restaurant workers. Moreover, Filipinos native skills and talent are further complemented with the hotel industry's in-house training programs. Moreover, employee performance is monitored and regularly evaluated using set working standards and performance criteria.

Finally, most local hotels are quick to respond to changes in technology. To date, most have computerized bookings, reservations, room service, and accounting systems.

Pressure on hotel prices comes from the drive "for value for money". Increased operating efficiency obtained through the computerization has helped to reduce costly waste in the supply chain. However, higher labour, raw materials, and utility costs continue to push operating costs up. Finally, in the macro level, economic and political factors affect the performance of the tourism industry. In the past two years, for example, declining disposable income resulting from the Asian currency crisis and political instability resulted in a 3% contraction in tourist arrivals in 1998 and a 1% increase in 1999.

Restaurants There are about 45,220 restaurant establishments in the domestic economy and about 80% of them belong to the fast food sub-sector. Food franchising is extremely popular. There are 1,057 franchised quick serve restaurants, 14 casual dining and theme restaurants, and 507 coffee shops, bakeries, and confectioneries.

U.S. firms have a very strong presence in the Philippine food franchising industry. As of 1998, in addition to McDonald's and Shakey's, other U.S. franchisees present in the market and their corresponding number of outlets are A&W (14); Burger King (10); Church's Fried Chicken (27); Domino's (17); Kenny Roger's Roasters (19); KFC (73); Pizza Hut (80); Sbarro (6); Subways (5); Wendy's (43); Bennigan's (1); California Pizza Kitchen (1); Hard Rock Cafe (1); Tony Roma's (1); Thai Barbecue (1); Outback (1); TGIF (4); Italianni's (2); Henry J. Bean (2); Baskin-Robbins (12); Dairy Queen (17); Dunkin' Donuts (424); Haagen-Daz (2); Mrs. Fields (12); Orange Julius (20); Starbucks (7); and TCBY (3).

Low barriers to entry characterize the industry. Capital investments particularly for franchises can range from PHP500,000 to PHP10,000. Training, marketing and distribution channels are arranged by the franchisor. Likewise, as the franchisor provides the new entrant fully developed management and production systems, prior knowledge and experience are not required of franchisees. These characteristics of franchising, particularly of food establishments, make the business very attractive for new entrepreneurs.

The proliferation of one-stop shopping malls that offer various recreational facilities and amenities, likewise, eases the entry of potential restaurant and fast food players. These malls spare the restaurant industry from spending extensive business development studies for their outlets; mall magnates Henry Sy and John Gokongwei Jr. have established formidable track records in building malls. The industry in which the restaurant and fast food firms operate has increasing consumer demand for every improving product. The growth is proven by the rapid expansion of food outlets in key areas in Metro Manila and the provinces. The popularity of fast food establishments came in the 1980's, and over the last years, the industry has consistently posted double-digit growth rates.

Competition is fierce in the restaurant industry, particularly the fast food sub-sector. The market is large but consumers are price conscious and exhibit brand loyalty. With a wide range of restaurants and fast food establishments to choose from, pricing schemes and marketing strategies determine market shares. Market strategies of industry players, therefore, aim to achieve two primary objectives: 1) hammer in "value-for-money" concepts; and 2) create brand consciousness and loyalty.

Market shares in the restaurants are won or lost in pricing. Industry players regularly offer price cuts and discounts to lure in new customers. Moreover, major players invest heavily in advertising to create brand consciousness and loyalty. Marketing strategies include raffle draws, free gift items and specially prized meal combinations, discounted toys and school items for every certain minimum food purchase. Celebrity endorsements are used in the hopes that the market will identify with the endorser.

Likewise, intense competition urges players to come up with new products to capture bigger market shares. Restauranteurs have to be keen at finding the latest food and wine concoctions here and abroad and adapting them to local taste. Targeting the Filipino's tastebuds, several fastfood chains that usually serve only western food have introduced items that appeal to the local market's palate.

Raising quality standards and improving service have also been focal points of competition, particularly in the fast food sub-sector. Players give incentives and compensations to motivate employees to be efficient on their jobs and thus help maintain the fast food outlet's high standards of quality service and cleanliness. Also, a major importance in a fast food and restaurant is courteous and friendly personnel. Not surprisingly, speedy service is among the more salient attributes people would highly expect from a fast food restaurant.

Finally, to keep their share of the market, food chains find it necessary to extend their service coverage by setting up other branches. Industry players who have outlets that are visible in Metro Manila and in other key urban cities are ones who are most likely to take in more profits. Malls, university areas, and other places where there is heavy pedestrian traffic are the usual places where fast food and restaurants are highly patronized.

Restaurant and fast food industry players balance their marketing concerns with the rising operation costs particularly that of imported food ingredients. Profit margin erosion is usually remedied by either increasing prices of final product/service or cut corners in production or the delivery of service. Either solution may result in a shrinking customer base.

In 1999, the 278 top restaurants in the Philippines posted a total of PHP33.7 billion in gross revenues, 8.6% higher than the 1998 PHP31 billion. Net income for the same firms, however, only increased slightly from PHP812 million in 1998 to PHP815 million the following year. Asset and equity investment likewise increased during the period by 32.7% and 52.3%, respectively.

Profitability for the top 181 firms also went down by 7.7% from 1998's 0.026 to 1999's 0.024 despite the industry's requirement of less capital, 0.102 unit in 1999 from 0.125 in 1998, to produce one extra unit of output.

In the fast food segment, Jollibee remains at the top with an estimated 29% share of the restaurant sub-sector's gross revenue in 1999 and about 50% market share of the local hamburger-segment patrons. Friendly service and a well-tailored, value-priced menu enable Jollibee to secure the domestic market. Its product iine caters to both sweet and spicy cuisine. Prices are relatively lower as compared to McDonald's, one of its closest rivals, making Jollibee affordable to those who belong to the lower-and middle-income brackets.

McDonald's, a distant second, accounts for about 28% of the local hamburger-segment patrons. McDonald's chains had to overcome the impression of being "too American". Thus, part of its marketing strategy is the "Filipinization" of its product line and service. McDonald's now uses the Filipino language in its stores. Moreover, the chain stores has adapted an expanded product line to include Filipino favourites such as spaghetti, fried chicken, and longganisa breakfast.

The local fine dining and speciality restaurants segment accounted for less than 15% of the restaurant sub-sector's 1999 gross revenue. Although top ten restaurant chains account for about 70% of the local fine dining segment market, the biggest player Perf Restaurants Inc. only ranked 9th, with a 1.6% of the total restaurant sub-sector's gross revenue.

In general, the restaurant industry's strength lies primarily in technology development. Technology transfer and franchising, allow interested parties to operate a franchise without prior experience or training. Domestic and international food chains and franchises facilitate transfer of technology in the local restaurant sub-sector. They provide training of potential employees and employ strict quality control systems. Raw materials are likewise provided by the franchisor.

Finally, there is no real threat of external substitutes to the services provided by the restaurant industry. Indeed, it is competition between the subsectors of the industry that determines market share.

Seasonality of Demand

Hotel. Demand for the hotel sub-sector's services, particularly that of accommodations, peak in the months of November, December and January. Foreign visitor arrivals are at its highest in the last and first months of the year, accounting, on the average, for 18% of the total. Peak season for balikbayan arrivals, on the other hand, is during the months of November and December, accounting for 36% of the total.

Restaurant. The restaurant industry is less cyclical than fast food chains. It lies in the fact that a relatively small percentage, probably less than 15% of the eating-out market, is accounted for by relatively high-priced meals. This sector is considered as a luxury segment of the eating out market. In contrast, eating out at fast food is adjunct either to shopping or employment and not really recreational.

For most part, majority of the industry's revenues is spread evenly over the fiscal year. However, the month of December is observed to have a significantly higher sales which can be attributed to the Christmas shopping and celebration of Christmas parties and dinner in big restaurants. In terms of weekly seasonality, height of business activity for a fast food chain would be weekends including the days (Friday and Monday) close to this time of the week. Data indicate that it is probable that more people eat out after going to Mass with Sunday representing the peak-day of the week when customer visit fast food outlets. Each working day (Monday to Friday) of the week is certain to attract a tenth of fast food customers.

External Support Systems

The presence of external support systems can enhance an industry's competitive advantage. Factor conditions (i.e., cost of capital, labour and raw materials), for example, are affected through subsidies, policies toward the capital markets, policies toward education, and the like. External support systems can also help stimulate local demand conditions, establish local product standards or regulations and programs that mandate or influence buyers' needs. The local hotel and restaurant industry external support systems include government agencies, industry associations and trade unions.

Government agencies and various consultative bodies, which includes but is not limited to the Department of Tourism, Department of Trade and Industry, Department of Labour and Employment, and the Hotel and Restaurant Tripartite Consultative Body, Inc., work together to promote the tourism and hotel and restaurant industries through specifically designed laws, policies and programs that promote industry growth and industrial peace, safeguard labour rights, provide training and seminars, and ensure consumer safety. Programs specifically designed to attract more tourists and therefore expand the hotel and restaurant industry's market, for example, is the DOT's Tourism Master Plan.

The Tourism Master Plan (TMP) is the framework and guide of the Department of Tourism for the sustained development and expansion of the tourism industry of the Philippines. Completed in 1991, it serves as the blueprint for tourism development in the country until the year 2010. The Plan was prepared by the Hoff and Overgaard on behalf of the World Tourism Organization (WTO), United Nations Development Program (UNDP) and the DOT. Its aim is to position the Philippines as a leading tourist destination in Asia. Its specific objectives are:

1. To increase the contribution of tourism economic growth at a national and regional level;
2. To enhance and contribute to social cohesion and cultural preservation at the local level;
3. To develop tourism on an environmentally sustainable basis; and 4. To develop a diversity of destinations, attractions and markets.

To achieve these objectives, the TMP identifies the following primary strategies for tourism development:

1. To establish three main destination clusters in Luzon, Visayas and Mindanao with Luzon to be positioned as a multi-faceted destination; Visayas as a resort and cultural heritage destination; and Mindanao as an exotic wilderness destination. Each cluster will have its own international airport and diverse satellite destinations.
2. To adopt a combination of niche and mass marketing approaches to target a wider base of the market; and
3. To develop international and domestic tourism. For the Luzon development cluster, the TMP has identified the northern portion of Palawan, including Puerto Princesa, as a priority tourism development area.

A copy of the law creating the Department of Tourism is found in Annex B and a description of the DOT's latest projects is described in Annex C. Industry associations, on the other hand, enable the hotel and restaurant sector, among other things, to undertake programs and projects that upgrade and professionalize the sector (i.e., training and seminars for employees and industry promotion by sponsoring domestic and international exhibits) and to influence government regulatory policies/laws/rules affecting the industry. A description of selected hotel and restaurant industry associations is found in Annex D.

Finally, trade unions in the hotel and restaurant industry, among other things, safeguard the rights and welfare of industry workers and professionals. They work closely with government and industry participants in improving working conditions and employee performance (i.e., recommending additional training and or certification) and in defending employee rights. Annex E gives a brief description of selected hotel and restaurant industry trade unions.

Forward Linkage/Market

Hotel. The most important buyers of hotel services are the tourists (domestic and foreign), the local consumers who dine in restaurants and institutions who use the function rooms for social and business purposes. Notwithstanding the currency and economic turmoil in Asia, the Philippine tourism industry posted 2.17 billion arrivals in 1999. The strong performance of the industry is attributed to the government's aggressive promotions in major travel markets and the high frequency of repeat visitors registered by the industry at 53%.

In the past five years, visitor arrivals have been growing at an annual average of 9%, contributing more than US$2.3 billion per year to the country's foreign exchange earnings. The months of January and December account for the greatest number of foreign visitor arrivals with a share of 18%. Auguring well for the industry during the period was the consistent monthly increase in arrivals, the highest of which was recorded in December, primarily accredited to the heavy influx of balikbayans eager to celebrate the coming of the new millenium in the Philippines.

Although overseas Filipino arrivals have been on a decline since 1994 from 159,169 to an all time low of 134,541 in 1997, balikbayan homecoming, however, picked up in 1998 to 174,277, posting a 29.5% increase. Thus, pulling the average growth rate for the period to 3.4%. Overseas Filipinos contributed an annual average of US$212.6 million to the country's foreign exchange earnings over the past six years. The peak season for balikbayan arrivals is the November to December period, accounting for 36% of the total.

Owing to the various political issues, visitor arrivals during the first nine months of the year 2000 fell 4.42%, 1.52 million from January to September as compared to the 1.57 million during the same period of 1999. Visitor receipts and length of stay likewise went down, 10.4% and 5.9%, respectively.

Meanwhile, in terms of market segmentation, the first semester 2000 figures show that the US continued to supply the biggest bulk of tourists, an estimated 23% of the inbound traffic followed by Japan at 20%. Other major source markets include Korea (8.3%), Hong Kong (7.3%), the United Kingdom (4%), Taiwan (3.6%), Australia (3.6%), Canada (3%), Germany (2.6%), and Singapore (2.3%). Overseas Filipinos accounted for about 7.3% of total visitor traffic. The Philippines enjoyed one of the highest repeat visits in Asia, 52.76% in September 2000.

The primary purpose of foreign visitors to the Philippines in September 2000 is holiday (41.7%), visit friends and family, (24%) and business (22%). An estimated 99% of all foreign visitors during the same period travelled by air with the balance coming in by sea. Majority, about 63%, is male and 35% are female, while the average age of all foreign visitors is 38.9 years old. The data on tourist arrivals also revealed that only an estimated 20% of foreign visitors availed of package tours. Majority, about 63%, made their own travel arrangements. Finally, on the average, foreign visitors spent US$113.67 per day in September 2000. The biggest expenditure being accommodations, 39%, and food and beverage 22%.

Hotels are the most popular source of accommodation among foreign travellers. In the past five years, more than 50% of foreign tourists used hotels for accommodations.

As foreign tourists are not very price sensitive, they are usually after the amenities and service that they need during their hectic travel. Hotels that cater to the tourist market compete mostly in the area of amenities and services. Local customers, on the other hand, can be further divided into individual and institutional patrons. Individual patrons (i.e., professionals, families, etc.) are price sensitive. Hotels, therefore, compete intensely with each other in terms of packages. During specific seasons of the year, hotels offer weekend and/or holiday packages (generally includes discounted accommodations and meals). These packages are also offered to specific market segments – wedding parties, honeymooners, and balikbayans.

Research shows that the following factors affect the foreign and domestic household consumers' decision in choosing hotels and other lodging facilities: 1) competitive or discounted "pricing"; 2) free services (i.e., local calls, children's toys & gifts, continental breakfast, etc.); and 3) services tailored to the needs of children (i.e., nightlight, pediatrician on-call services, swimming pool with lifeguard, children's menu in hotel restaurants and child friendly or safe room).

Institutional patrons include company-sponsored employee training programs, seminars, and workshops. Different sub-sectors of the wholesale and retail industry are well-known for conducting marketing and promotional activities in various local hotels (i.e., computer, hardware and software, promotion, large-scale office equipment manufacturers, for example Xerox, etc.). Other important markets include the non-ferrous smelting and refining plants sector (18%), public administration and defence (17.4%), and finance (11.6%) industries.

Nonetheless, despite the above efforts, local hotels are still not able to capture a significant share of the domestic tourist market. The patronage of domestic tourists ensures the survival and profitability of most businesses that are dependent upon tourism primarily because domestic tourists outnumber foreign visitors. In the Philippines, 80% of all tourists are domestic travellers; their total spending, tourists who are at least 18 years old, amounts to about PHP57 billion. Very few hotel operators, however, are able to tap into this market. Price conscious, most domestic travellers depend on family and friends to arrange trips and provide lodging.

Restaurant. The restaurant industry caters to both household and institutional buyers. The Philippine household market is segmented into five income groups (A, B, C, D and E). Based on the preliminary results of the 1997 Family Income and Expenditure Survey (FIES), the middle income bracket has expanded from the 1994 level.

The table above shows that families have experienced improvements in their income in 1997 from 1994, which indicates an increase in the local population's buying power. Furthermore, FIES data show that spending on food consumed outside the home has been increasing from 3.1%in 1985 to 4.7% in 1997. With total family expenditures increasing more than four times during the period, this translated to more than PHP66.8 billion spent on restaurant services in 1997.

As their workload increased, the change in spending pattern reflects the Filipino families' growing propensity to take advantage of the convenience offered by fast food and restaurants in the area of food preparation. With the growth in income and expenditure over time, however, the spending pattern of Filipino families is slowly shifting from food to non-food consumption. In 1997, for example, the share of food expenditures to total expenditures amounted to 43.9%, 3.9% points lower than the 1994 proportion.

Demographically, Philippine consumer market is a large one, approximately 75 million Filipinos. The profile of the local population consists of 65% youth (ages 0-29), 29% mature (30-59), 6% senior citizens (ages 60 and above).

For the youth, which dominates the local market in terms of numbers, eating out is a regular activity. Key factors that make fast food establishments attractive to this group include the simplicity of food preparation, high quality of food served in a clean, orderly environment, prompt service and relatively inexpensive prices.

Other markets consist of families who make weekend dining an occasion and professionals in urban centres who opt to eat-out during office breaks, especially on pay days.

The pricing of company's goods and services must be competitive due to the generic nature of its products. In turn, fast food establishments respond by introducing new products and special offers. It has embarked on "value meals", a popular marketing strategy which features a combination menu that offers a customer a little of everything at a discounted price. On the other hand, restaurants have followed suit, applying a similar strategy, the "Eat-All-You-Can", where a customer enjoys a sumptuous meal for half the price, with the condition of "no leftovers". Another strategy of fast food outlets is a 50% discount before the closing time.

Finally, recent studies show that Filipino consumers value the following characteristics of restaurant products and services as the most important, according to priority:

1) flavor and taste;
2) value for money/nutrient content;
3) presentation and packaging;
4) variety;
5) systematic ordering and selling;
6) feeling of security in food and environment;
7) prompt delivery and service;
8) consistency of service;
9) feeling of recognition and importance; and
10) feeling of security in location and accessibility.

Meanwhile, institutional buyers employ the services of the restaurant industry for occasions such as seminars, workshops, meetings, company celebrations, and marketing and promotional activities. Among the hotel and restaurant industry's main institutional markets are the wholesale and retail trade (30.4%), air transport (23%), and the other recreational and cultural services sectors (5.7%).

Backward Linkage/Suppliers

Hotel. Suppliers of majority of hotel inputs are many. Hoteliers are therefore able to scout for the best inputs at reasonable prices. In most cases, suppliers are even the ones who send brochures and quotations to hotels for possible contracts.

At any rate, most hotels have arrangements with their respective accredited suppliers, in particular, of food and beverage products. Imported supplies command a premium, but deluxe and first-class hotels are willing to pay for high quality. Supplies and raw materials for restaurants operated by hotels account for about 19% of the hotel industry's operating cost, ocean, coastal and inland fishing sector (11.3%) and softdrinks and carbonated water sector (7.6%). Other major suppliers of the hotel industry include, power (10.6%), the perfumes, cosmetics and toilet preparations (6.8%), and wholesale and retail (5.3%) industries.

Meanwhile, imports supply more than 90% of the Philippine hotel and restaurant equipment market. In 1998, imports were estimated at US$70.39 million, registering an 18.5 percent drop from 1997 imports of US$97.35 million. In general, imported equipment consist of refrigerating or freezing display counters and showcases, machinery for making hot drinks or for cooking or heating food, not normally used in the household, dishwashing machines, laundry-type washing machines exceeding 10 kgs., dry-cleaning machines, and automatic vending machines.

The U.S. remains the largest source of imported equipment in 1998 with a 45% market share. End-users prefer American-made equipment because of excellent quality, durability, and users' familiarity with them. Manufacturers from Japan (14%), Europe (12%), Korea (6%) and Singapore (4%) also supplied the import market.

After the U.S., Japanese suppliers sold US$11.34 million worth of equipment with a 14% import market share, followed by Korea with sales of US$5.04 million and a 6% import market share, and Singapore with US$3.37 million sales and a 4% market share. The European countries led by Germany, Denmark, Italy, and Netherlands had a 12% import market share and sales of US$10.13 million.

Japan's import market share jumped from 9% in 1997 to 14% in 1998. Japanese suppliers trailed the U.S. in sales of refrigerating/ freezing display counters, cabinets and showcases; other refrigerating equipment; and drycleaning

machines. Korea proved to be strong in sales of automatic goods/vending machines, while Singapore suppliers were effective in sales of machinery for making hot drinks/for cooking/and heating food, as well as other refrigerating equipment. The dominant European suppliers were the Germans, Danish, Dutch, and Italian.

These suppliers shared the market for refrigerating and freezing display counters, equipment for making hot drinks, and washing, bleaching/dyeing machines with U.S. suppliers and the other third-country suppliers. In particular, Italian coffee/espresso machines were the leaders in this field. European equipment is popular in deluxe and first class hotels because of the presence of European chefs.

Local production, on the other hand, is limited to basic food service and kitchen equipment. Major local suppliers of stainless kitchen equipment such as counters, refrigeration equipment, and ovens include Fab-Asia, Allied Metals, Inc., and Gomeco Metal Corporation. Lowtemp Corp. manufactures refrigerated equipment; Pacific Star International Sales, stainless and galvanized iron furniture; Almedah Food Machineries Corp., rice grinders, hotdog rollers, convection ovens, fish ball forming/makers; meat grinders; emulsifiers; and Optima Systems, food showcases.

Liberalization is expected to reduce the bargaining power of suppliers further. At present, for example, a 10% tariff rate is imposed on imported hotel and restaurant equipment. The reduction and the eventual removal of tariff rates on hotel equipment, therefore, will allow more hoteliers to either replace or add to their current equipment. Making local establishment more attractive to both local and foreign patrons.

Likewise, deregulating the transport sector, one of the industry's major suppliers will significantly reduce transportation rates, benefiting hotel operators around the country. Moreover, with liberalization, improvements in technology developed in one country are shared automatically with other countries. They are shared directly when they are embodied in new capital equipment that would relatively be cheaper with the reduction/removal of tariff and non-tariff barriers. As with other industries, the hotel sub-sector would benefit from the availability of cheaper and more modern technology (i.e., hotel systems such as reservations, accounting, etc.).

Finally, liberalization will allow the free movement and employment of international hotel managers, chefs, cooks and other hotel-related professions in the country.

Restaurant. Because of limited supply or lack of substitutes, suppliers have substantial influence over pricing of goods and services. Supplier power for the fast food industry is high because the number of food manufacturers is not enough to cater to the rapidly growing demand of food chains in their daily consumption needs. This strong demand for food supply from the big food manufacturing companies is a result of the increasing number of fast food chains in the Philippines.

Most players prefer to get their raw materials locally. They negotiate directly with producers, manufacturers and wholesale distributors for food, beverage and packaging products to ensure the freshness of food products, for a uniform quality and to obtain competitive prices. However, industry players get two of their most basic raw materials abroad, namely beef and french fries. Beef is imported from Australia and french fries from the United States and other countries because the local supply of beef is insufficient there is virtually no potato industry.

Among the concerns of fast food establishments in their choice of suppliers are prices, substitution of raw materials, freshness and uniform quality. Among the industry's biggest suppliers are the slaughtering and meat packing (27.5%), rice and corn milling (7.4%), and ocean, coastal, and inland fishing (5.9%) sub-sectors.

The emergence of free trade will certainly affect most industries today, including the fast food and restaurant industries. The General Agreement on Tariffs and Trade/World Trade Organization (GATT/WTO) would be a challenge to the fast food industry because local suppliers would have to be more competitive given the different suppliers coming into the local market.

Laws Hindering/Facilitating

Hotel. In 1995, the Ramos administration signed Executive Order No. 219 establishing the domestic and international civil aviation liberalization policy. It opened domestic routes to competition and designated at least two international carriers as official carriers for the Philippines. According to the E.O., the government should pursue national interest and not the interest of only one carrier.

The liberalization policy was adopted to address the urgent need for the Philippines to improve air service availability, equality and efficiency through exposure to foreign markets and competition. This liberalization policy was consistent with the thrust to expand investment and trade by increasing air access for Filipino as well as foreign passengers.

When the domestic market was opened to competition, new players came in. They were Cebu Pacific, Air Philippines, Asian Spirit and Mindanao Express. They provided additional seats, lower prices and proved that the so-called "missionary routes" can be financially viable.

In 1995, when PAL was the only local carrier, only six million seats were available for domestic travellers. By 1999, there were ten million seats available, a 67% growth in air access to various destinations in the Philippines.

Contrary to claims by PAL that there was no market, these figures revealed that there was unserved demand for local travel. From two million in 1995, passenger traffic more than doubled by 1999.

Competition, likewise, made travel more affordable. In 1995, a roundtrip ticket in the Manila-Cebu route used to cost PHP2,846. In 1999, this was reduced to PHP2,598. Indeed, on the average roundtrip ticket prices to Cebu, Davao, and Zamboanga from Manila went down by 39.56%, the biggest reduction being on the Manila-Zamboanga-Manila route, 47.71%. Competition also proved that there are really no "missionary routes". Niche airlines such as Asian Spirit, Mindanao Express and SEAIR provide now service to tertiary routes which PAL abandoned in 1998. Both Asian Spirit and SEAIR, for instance, operate in Busuanga. These smaller carriers proved that these tertiary routes can be financially viable. Load factors in Busuanga and Masbate reached 70% and 76%, respectively in 1998.

The liberalization of international airline service (which increased access and reduced cost of travel) complemented the worldwide economic growth of the 1990s. The Philippine international tourism, in particular, gained from these developments as evidenced by the increasing growth in tourist arrivals during the period 1994-2000. Tourist arrivals to the Philippines increased by more than 37%, from 1.6 in 1994 to 2.2 in 1999. The growth in arrivals translated to higher receipts for the economy, from US$2.28 billion in 1994 to US$2.55 billion in 1999, or a 12% increase.

Moreover, liberalization made possible the direct links between Northeast Asian cities and Cebu, thus, making Cebu more accessible, with cheaper fares. Consequently, incoming international passengers to Cebu went up by more than 23%, from 130,000 in 1994 to 160,000 in 1998. The Japanese market accounts for 34% of total visitor arrivals in Cebu, followed by the US (13%) and the Taiwanese (11%).

For the hotel and restaurant industry, therefore, E.O. 219 proved to be extremely beneficial. The reduction in transportation cost and the increase in airline destinations encouraged both domestic and international travels. The 2001 Investment Priorities Plan is formulated to serve as a conduit in the continuation of the economic reform programs crucial in sustaining the economic gains we have so far achieved. The implementation of these programs has ushered a continuous industrial development as evidenced by a strong growth of the industrial output, notable increase in foreign direct investments, acceleration of export sales, dispersal of growth to the countryside and congruent improvements in specific sectors.

For the past years, the annual drafting of the IPP has been guided by preceding economic development plans that include:

- the E.O. 226, otherwise known as the Omnibus Investments Code of the Philippines that specifies the incentives provided to priority investments; and
- the Medium-Term Philippine Development Plan of the Philippines (MTPDP) 1993-1998 that provides the agri-industrial vision for the country.

For this year, the 2001 IPP is, in part, being made parallel to the newly mandated Industrial Development Plan of the Philippines (IDPP), the blueprint for enhancing and sustaining global competitiveness of the Philippine industries in the short (1-

3 years), medium (4-10 years) and long (11-15 years) term. The 2001 IPP will provide incentives to qualified activities in the IDPP. Otherwise, other types of assistance including those not specified in the IPP will be rendered.

Furthermore, the 2001 IPP specifically lends support to the pursuance of the national development vision focusing on agri-industrial development, sustainable human development, science and technology, and environment and natural resources management.

To achieve continuation of programs, the general goals of the 2001 IPP shall encompass those specified under the past IPPs that include:

1) enhancement of global competitiveness;
2) increase in exports;
3) increase in agricultural productivity;
4) setting-up and upgrading of infrastructure and support facilities;
5) countryside development;
6) alleviation of poverty through the creation of employment opportunities and the reduction in the cost of living;

In addition, the 2001 IPP will also cover the goals of the IDPP necessary in directing the country towards sustained growth and competitiveness:

1) improvement of the science and technology competence and support to the R& D efforts in industries;
2) assistance to SMEs by promoting linkage between the SMEs and large industries steering them in the direction of advanced technology and high value-added products; and,
3) ensuring efficient environment and energy management.

The 2001 IPP will, likewise, maintain the industry classifications previously laid-down in the past IPP's, to wit:

1) Export-Oriented Activities

2) Catalytic Industries
3) Industries Undergoing Industrial Adjustments
4) Support Industries
5) Mandatory Inclusions.

Thirteen (13) economic activities are listed in this year's plan. The modernization program with a possible three-year income tax holiday will continue to be made available in the 2001 IPP. However, as a step closer to our objective of achieving social equity, support to projects uplifting the welfare of the consuming public will be reinforced. Projects identified under the Social Reform Agenda of the government which include socialized/low cost housing projects and other social services such as the establishment of educational/ training institutions, rehabilitation centres, health service facilities, and new retirement villages will be given priority.

Moreover, the 2001 IPP shall continue its commitment to encourage the establishment of Research and Development projects in an effort to fast track the development of technology in the country and the introduction of innovative products and processes in the market. As one of the basic economic sectors in the country, the acceleration of agricultural productivity will be propelled through the provision of continued support to the key areas identified in the Agriculture and Fishery Modernization Act by promoting integration of processes and activities to ensure food security and encourage more value-adding.

The 2001 IPP is likewise formulated as a component of the overall economic development plan that is responsive to the country's commitments under formal trade and investment agreements such as the AFTA, APEC and WTO.

Policy and legislative measures are continuously being initiated towards the rationalization of the incentives scheme that will strike a balance between the provision of sector-specific and time-bound incentives attuned to the needs and peculiarities of strategic sectors and the universalization of substantive incentives across all industries. Once these measures are in place, activities listed in the IPP will be limited to a few critical industries that will accord optimum economic gains on a long-term basis. In addition to the national listing of the 2001 IPP is a special listing of economic activities identified for promotion and eligible for incentives by the Autonomous Region for Muslim Mindanao (ARMM). The ARMM IPP is the list of priority areas that have been independently determined by the Regional Board of Investments (RBOI) of the ARMM in accordance with E.O. 458. Economic activities in this special listing shall be pursued in the ARMM only. However, economic activities listed in the national IPP may have its location also inside the ARMM.

In particular, among other sub-sector beneficiaries, the provisions above apply to the following sub-sectors in the tourism industry:

- tourist accommodation facilities which refer to hotel, apartel, tourist inns, pension house, and resorts. Resorts may also include special interest activities (which may or may not have accommodation facilities) such as but not limited to theme parks, convention, exhibition/trade display centres, eco-tourism projects or those involving environmentally sound tourism activities in a given ecosystem yielding socioeconomic benefits and enhancing natural and cultural diversity conservation.
- tourism estates which refer to large tracts of land with defined boundaries in any of the destination areas in the country, suitable for development into an integrated complex with prescribed carrying capacities of tourist facilities and activities such as but not limited to accommodation, food and recreational centres and commercial outlets, and provided with roads, water supply facilities, power distribution facilities, drainage and sewerage systems and other necessary infrastructure.
- tourist buses
- restoration of historical and cultural sites/properties provided that the sites/properties are at least 100 years old as certified by the National Historical Institute and endorsed by the Department of Tourism. A copy of the 2001 IPP and its implementing guidelines are found in Annex F of this study.

Meanwhile, employment of foreign nationals in the industry is subject to a tripartite agreement promulgated in 1992 between the Department of Tourism (DOT) and Department of Labour and Employment (DOLE) and the Bureau of Immigration (BI). The agreement addresses the following issues regarding the employment of foreign nationals in the hotel and restaurant industry: positions open to foreign nationals, procedures in the issuance of visa/permits, and disciplinary/penal provisions.

According to the agreement, only hotels and resorts duly licensed by the DOT shall be allowed to engage the services of foreign nationals. Foreign nationals in hotels and resorts that are already operational may occupy a maximum of four (4) managerial positions. Hotels or resorts yet to be constructed may employ as many foreign nationals as may be required during the stage of construction and up to six (6) months after opening of the hotel to the public. Moreover, the services of foreign nationals may be availed of during special occasions/events such as food festivals; provided, however, that the service contract shall be limited to a period of three (3) months renewable for a maximum period of another three (3) months.

A pre-requisite for employment of foreign nationals in the hotel and resort sub-sectors is a pre-arranged employment visa from the appropriate Philippine Embassy or Consulate or other designated visa-issuing office nearest their port of origin. If the foreign national has already been admitted into the country as a temporary visitor or under any other admission category, he may secure a change of status to pre-arranged employment visa from the Bureau of Immigration.

In the grant of the appropriate visa, the Department of Foreign Affairs and the Bureau of Immigration shall generally endeavor to determine non-work connected qualifications of the applicant.

As a pre-requisite to the issuance of the pre-arranged employment visa or change of status, the foreign national applicant shall secure an Alien Employment Permit from DOLE, which shall grant the same on the basis of nonavailability of the services of local expertise for the vacancy, the undertaking of an understudy training program as appropriate, and in compliance with its other policy guidelines.

Finally, any person who violates the provisions outlined in the agreement shall be subject to any of the following penalties:

1. A fine of not less than PHP1,000 but not more than PHP10,000 or imprisonment of not less than three (3) months, or both as provided for by Article 289 of the Labour Code;
2. Non-renewal of the Alien Employment Permit and/or visa;
3. Suspension or revocation of the Alien employment Permit;
4. Deportation.

Restaurant. The government has taken an active role in cultivating an environment that would allow the local fast food industry to be globally competitive and to operate at levels comparable to international standards. Specifically, the Department of Health (DOH), together with the Bureau of Food and Drugs (BFAD) are directed to ensure strict food quality and hygiene standards. Under the new Intellectual Property (IP) Act, the Bureau of Patents, Trademarks and Technology Transfer (BPTTT) has been abolished. IP has been created to assume the BPTTT's functions of authorizing the registration of trademarks, service marks and other marks of ownership, hear and preside over proceedings affecting rights to trademarks. Meanwhile, the Department of Trade and Industry (DTI) is the governing agency that approves various promotions and advertisement campaigns of fast food chains.

All franchise agreements with foreign franchisors are registered with IP as well as licensing, technical assistance and services, technology transfer and distribution agreements.

Foreign franchisors in the Philippines, similar to other industries, are subject to the restrictions on ownership, 40%. The laws on technology transfer, however, guarantee franchisors in the Philippines royalties of 5% and a maximum allowable term of technology transfer arrangements of ten years. Finally, as with the hotel and resort sub-sector, foreign national employment in the restaurant sub-sector is subject to the tripartite agreement signed by the Department of Tourism, Department of Labour and Employment and the Bureau of Immigration.

Speciality restaurants are allowed to employ foreign nationals subject to the following conditions:

Only speciality restaurants duly accredited with the DOT as well as those forming part of the integrated operation of licensed hotels/resorts may be allowed to engage the services of foreign nationals;

A speciality restaurant with a minimum seventy-five (75) seat capacity shall be allowed to have one (1) foreign Speciality Chef or Sous Chef. In the initial stage of operation of a speciality restaurant and for a maximum period of two (2) years, three (3) more foreign speciality chefs or sous chefs may be allowed;

A speciality restaurant with a seating capacity of 500 or more may be allowed to employ three (3) additional foreign nationals in any of the following positions:

(a) as speciality chef(s);

(b) as sous chef(s);

(c) as food service manager (s); or

(d) a combination of the above.

A foreign national may be allowed to replace a Filipino citizen who is assigned to work abroad on a training program and who is presently occupying one of the positions that can be filled by foreign nationals under the agreement; provided, however, that in no case shall the foreign national be allowed to stay beyond two (2) years or the duration of the training of the Filipino, whichever, comes first.

The same policies are followed regarding the procedures in the issuance of visa/permits and disciplinary/penal provisions as the hotel and resort sub-sector.

Market Potential/Foreign Market Demand and Competition

Local hotel and restaurant players can enter the foreign market through any of three modes of supply: 1) cross-border supply/

consumption abroad; 2) commercial presence; and 3) movement of natural persons. Foreigners coming to the Philippines is classified under the first mode, cross-border supply while Filipino-owned enterprises setting-up branches abroad through franchising (i.e., Jollibee, Goldilocks, Barrio Fiesta, etc.) is classified under the second mode.

Transfer of technology through franchising, however, is subject to the unique laws of the market the hotel and restaurant firms intend to penetrate. These laws, which are as varied as the countries that implement them, commonly address issues such as royalties, repatriation of profits, employment of foreign nationals, property ownership, taxes, and the like. Finally, the international deployment of hotel and restaurant workers and professionals is classified under the third mode, movement of natural persons. It is subject to laws pertaining to the practice of their profession. Indeed, most countries have policies preventing foreign professionals from practicing their profession in the domestic market.

Extent of Services Rendered Abroad

Export of services in the hotel and restaurant industry takes the form of sending industry workers and professionals to work for establishments belonging to the sector in a foreign land.

In the last five years, hotel and restaurant related workers and professional deployment averaged more than 6,740 per year. An estimated 75% of all hotel and restaurant professionals deployed during the period were cooks, waiters, bartenders and other related workers.

Filipino hotel and restaurant workers and professionals are known for their competence, trainability, and ease in adapting to different environments and are, therefore, in demand in the international market. Most hotel and restaurant related workers and professionals during the five-year period were deployed to United Arab Emirates, Saudi Arabia, Kuwait, Papua New Guinea, Singapore Malaysia, and the United States.

Moreover, large Filipino communities abroad are strong basis for the export of local restaurants and fast food technology. The presence of Goldilocks, Jollibee, Max, Red Ribbon, and Barrio

Fiesta, among others, in the US, for example, is a result of demand from Filipino migrants longing for a taste for home.

Foreign Market Demand and Competition

Hotels. The Philippines still lags behind in terms of tourist arrivals. The 1997 peak tourist arrival of 2.2 million pales in comparison with country leaders such as France with 70 million and Spain with 47.7 million. In Southeast Asia, country leaders, such as Hong Kong and Thailand, attract as much as 11 to 7 million visitors per year.

Moreover, data show that frequent travellers in Asia average 15 airline round trips each year and stay an exceptional 50 or more nights in hotels as compared to the Philippines average of 10 nights. As for the number of visitor arrivals from within the Asia Pacific, in 1999, the Philippines only placed ahead of Vietnam at 1.78 million. Competition with Vietnam and the Mekong Basin, however, is expected to intensify as the latter countries step up the promotion of their cluster as the holiday and convention destination in Asia in the 21st century.

Restaurant. Growing prosperity in Europe and the US promises steady growth in the percentage of meals eaten in restaurants. The greatest strength will be in the fast food and other economy restaurants, which offer convenience for increasingly hurried two-income families, and expensive restaurants known for quality, which offer an affordable taste of luxury. Mid-prices restaurants will find it difficult to compete.

Restaurants and food companies also adapt. McDonald's all 4,700 restaurants in the Pacific use Asian currencies for their business transactions. In Indonesia, it costs 80% less to build each restaurant due to lower costs for labour, real estate and other expenses. In Singapore, using local currencies, restaurants buy chicken patties from Thailand, rather than from the US, at much lower cost. The discussion below focuses on the performance of and the latest trend in the restaurant industry in eight major world markets: France, Italy, UK, US, Germany, Spain, Japan, and Canada.

The Japan and the United States are by far the largest consumer restaurant markets in the world, each valued at over US$200 billion in 1997. In Europe, Spain is the only market to exceed US$50 billion, well ahead of Italy, the UK and Germany. The smallest of the eight key markets is Canada, valued at just US$20 billion, reflecting a small and geographically widespread population.

Recent performance of the consumer catering market has varied across the major markets, as weak consumer confidence in several markets has impacted spending on non-essential items, and strengthening recovery in others has combined with more hectic lifestyles to boost demand for high quality, quick service meals and snacks.

Markets such as France, the UK and Japan have experienced further concentration in the consumer catering market as outlet numbers decline. The UK, however, highlights growing consumer confidence and the increasing popularity of dining out, as the slight decline in outlet numbers is more than matched by positive real value growth in 1997. Germany continues to be beset by economic recession and a heightened focus on the concept of value-formoney, and the only impetus for growth appears to come from new outlets. Thus the number of outlets rose in 1997, whilst market value declined in real and nominal terms.

Both Japan and the US have a greater number of restaurant outlets, respectively 915,752 and 706,600 in 1997, than either Canada or the European countries, and in the US the number of consumer catering outlets showed consistently positive growth over the review period. In contrast to the rise in outlet numbers in Italy, the US, Germany, Spain and Canada over the review period, there was a contraction of 3.8%, 2.3% and 1.3% in numbers in France, Japan and the UK respectively.

With an increase of 25.2% in outlet numbers over the period 1993-1997, Spain has increasingly adopted European-wide trends in the consumer catering market. Initially, a strong cultural identity in terms of culinary preferences hindered the progress of European and US-style fast food trends. However, the emergence of fast food outlets offering Spanish-based products has enlivened the market and boosted outlet numbers.

In France and the UK, however, competition and rationalization reduced outlet numbers over the period, but this process of consolidation appears to be slowing, with the rate of closures in the UK decreasing noticeably in 1997.

Traditional sectors have been the hardest hit by changing social and eating habits, with the rise in snacking and demand for convenience playing into the hands of fast food operators, which by the very nature of their operations meet the needs of consumers living faster-paced lifestyles.

The homogenization of European culture and internationalization of cuisine generally has also impacted consumer catering, as operators with the necessary flexibility to adapt to meet these demands achieve notable success. The 12% increase in outlet numbers in Canada over the period 1993-1997 reflects one aspect of the defensive strategies employed by consumer catering operators to ensure economic survival. In addition to menu diversification and co-branding, Canadian operators have chosen to expand the number of sites.

While traditional sectors have contracted as markets have consolidated, there have been pockets of growth. The Mediterranean restaurants have emerged as a popular consumer restaurant concept, as consumers are treated to a dining out experience, which extends far beyond a simple meal offer. The maintenance of high standards of quality and service, allied in some cases to value-for-money price points, have made such outlets popular eating places for families and business people.

Meanwhile, sales growth rates in the eight key markets varied considerably over the period 1993-1997, with nominal value growth registered in all the markets with the notable exception of Germany. Spain recorded the strongest value performance in nominal terms where restaurant sales increased by 24.4% over the five-year period. This growth translates into real value growth of some 7% for the same period and reflects the growing acceptance of the fast food concept, albeit with an Iberian slant. Tourism, both domestic and incoming, the popularity of meal vouchers and expansion of theme restaurants and bars targeting high-spending groups of consumers generally have buoyed the market. Competition and the rise of fast food catering have, however, undermined value growth as consumers come to expect lower price points.

The Canadian market recorded the strongest real value growth, where nominal growth of 23.5% translated into healthy real value growth of 16.9% for the period 1993-1997. A relatively strong economy and improved consumer confidence have fuelled eating out trends. Furthermore, operators have attempted to encourage greater premium purchases, remaining mindful, however, of the aging of the population and changing consumer base.

Stronger economic growth underpinned the healthy performance of both the US and the UK markets, resulting in real value growth of 7.7% and 5.2% respectively for the five-year review period. The convenience of good quality food through quick service outlets has driven value sales in the US, while the introduction of multi-concept restaurant chains has limited operator risk by appealing to a number of different sectors. In the UK, hectic lifestyles and the growth of tourism have boosted the frequency of eating out. The market has been further buoyed by the popularity of branded/theme outlets, particularly in the pubs sector.

Japan is the only remaining market to have registered real value growth over the review period, albeit a very modest 1%. In spite of ongoing economic difficulties there is a high incidence of eating out, but competition and lower spending confidence have forced operators to lower prices and accept tighter margins. The Japanese market has been further impacted by recent food health scares (most importantly the 0-157 bacillus), which have fundamentally changed the way consumers perceive consumer catering and the products offered.

Although both Italy and France registered nominal value growth over the period 1993-1997, this failed to translate into real value growth, resulting in declines of 7.6% and 7% respectively. The Italian market was particularly harshly hit by economic recession during the early part of the review period. Price has therefore become an important factor in the choice of catering outlet and the market as a whole has been unable to react swiftly to changing consumer demand. Traditional outlets have suffered especially, and the success of outlets offering innovative service at economical prices has failed to offset losses in the traditional restaurants sector.

French market value has been undermined by a series of negative influences, namely recession in 1993, terrorist attacks in 1995 and BSE scares in 1996. Business activity and tourism suffered as a consequence, although a recovery in 1997 was evident with a rise in the number of foreign visitors. Current lifestyles demand rapid service with high quality products and reasonable prices, factors which have further constrained price development.

The weakest performer of the major markets has been Germany, as the restaurant market has suffered value decline in both nominal and real terms. Average meal prices have declined as the influence of fast food and self-service has grown. The market reached its nadir in 1996 and appeared to have turned a corner in 1997, as operators proved more adept at dealing with and responding to the recession. As a result, outlet numbers are rising and consumers are being presented with a wider range of low/mid-price menus.

Supply Capability

Generally, hotels offer two major types of services: (a) accommodation and (b) dining services. Based on the quality and extent of services provided, location, bedroom, front office/ reception, food and beverage, general facilities (service and staff), and special facilities (i.e., business centre, limousine services and airport transfers), hotels are further classified as Deluxe, First Class, Standard, and Economy. Hotel guests can expect a room with private bath, telephone, radio, and television, in addition to such customer services such as laundry, valet, cleaning and pressing. Aside from the services mentioned, hotels have other facilities: function rooms, ballrooms, health spas, coffee shops, dining rooms, cocktail lounges or night clubs, gift shops or newsstand-tobacco counters, and business centres for social occasions, health buffs, and business conferences.

The restaurant industry, on the other hand, covers fine dining speciality restaurants, fast food outlets, canteens, and food courts. Fine dining and speciality restaurants offer a wide variety of international cuisines. The restaurant originated in France dating back to 1765 when one A. Boulanger, a soup vendor, opened an establishment advertising restoratives, or restaurants, referring to the soups and broths available within.

The institution took its name from the advertisement, and "restaurant" now denotes a public eating place in English, French, Dutch, Danish, Norwegian, Romanian, and many other languages, with some variations. In the Philippines, a new trend in the restaurant industry is rapidly gaining popularity, that is, "eat-all-you-can buffets", which are offered at reasonable prices. A number of restaurants offer "buffets with no leftovers" at 50% off normal buffet prices.

The cafeteria, an American contribution to the restaurant's development originated in San Francisco during the 1849 gold rush. Featuring self-service, it offers a wide variety of foods displayed on counters.

The customer makes his selections, paying for each item as he chooses it or paying for the entire meal at the end of the line. Other types of quick-eating places originating in the United States are the drugstore counter, serving sandwiches or other snacks; the lunch counter, where the diner is served a limited quick-order menu at the counter; and the "drive-through" or drive-up restaurant where patrons are served in their automobiles.

So-called fast food restaurants, usually operated in chains or as franchises and heavily advertised, offer limited menus-typically comprising of hamburgers, hot dogs, fried chicken, or pizza and their complements – likewise originated in the United States. Fast foods have the advantage of speed, convenience, and familiarity to diners who may eat in the restaurant or take their food home.

More than just as a place to eat, fast food consumers, however, may also avail themselves of party, such as birthdays and office celebration packages, and delivery services. Year-round party packages are offered by fast food chains, which generally include the venue, food, party games and give-a-ways. Delivery services, on the other hand, peak at lunchtime while night orders peak between the hours of 10 p.m. to 2 a.m.

Areas of Specialization

The industry as a whole does not have any particular expertise. Within the hotel sub-sector, however, players exert effort to develop niches in the market through product differentiation. The Westin Philippine Plaza, due to its proximity to the convention centre and target marketing, has cornered a large share of local and international business conferences and cultural events. Hotels in the Makati area, Hotel Intercon, Shangri-la, and the Ayala Hotels, in particular, are strong contenders in the business executives market.

Located in the premier commercial district of the capital, these hotels specialize in meeting the demands of business travellers. Hotel Intercom, for example, capitalized on its ideal location and deliberately put in place amenities and facilities to suit the changing needs of the business traveler.

Some of these eventually became the standard followed by other hotels here and abroad. Among these innovations are the Guest Net (enables all guests to access the Internet on their television screen through a wireless keyboard), Business Rooms ("mini offices" equipped with, among others, a large desk, a 5-in-1 copier/scanner/phone/fax/printer unit, and basic office amenities like pen and paper), and the cyberrelations officers (trained staff dedicated to helping guests with technical difficulties in operating their laptops or desktop computers).

In the restaurant sub-sector, market niching is likewise a practice. Top ten players in the restaurant sub-sector accounts for more than 70% of the total market. Max's Inc., the undisputed industry leader cornering almost 50% of the market, specializes in affordable family-type affairs/occasions (i.e., baptisms, birthday parties, and weddings). Aristocrat chains, that competes in the same segment, is not too far behind at 20%. Relatively new entrants such as Friday's and California Pizza Kitchen, taps into the young urban professionals market. In the fast food sub-sector, Jollibee is the undisputed market leader in the hamburger segment with a 50%. The chain appeals to the lower-to middleincome brackets with its relatively low prices and a menu that has successfully captured the Filipino tastebuds. McDonald's, with its relatively higher prices, is in second place with a 20% market share. The American fast food chain appeals to the AB crowd. Other hamburger fast food chains include Wendy's, which appeals to the relatively health conscious consumers and the pioneer in fast food delivery services, Burger Machine, catering mostly to travellers with its mobile restaurants in numerous gas stations, and Tropical Hut, mostly open 24-hours.

Relatively new players are Burger King and Carl's Junior, which resurfaced in the late nineties after pulling out in the early part of the decade. Meanwhile, the industry leaders in the pizza segment are Pizza Hut, Shakey's, Domino's Pizza, and Little Ceasar's, the newest entrant to the pizza market. Leaders in the pizza segment cater to the young adult crowd, particularly Shakey's pizza. In the chicken segment, Kentucky Fried Chicken is the undisputed market leader. Finally, only two establishments actively compete in the doughnut segment, Dunkin Donuts and Mister Donut. The former, Dunkin Donut leads with more than a 90% share. Doughnuts in the Philippines are usually consumed between meals rather than during breakfast, which is the case in the United States.

Expertise/Technical Competence of Manpower

Competent Filipino hotel and restaurant workers and professionals are one of the strengths of the hotel and restaurant industry. Filipinos are among the best-educated and most trainable people in Asia. They are capable of performing even the most complicated task with world-class competence. Filipino hotel employees are reputed to possess the following characteristics, which give local hotels an advantage over their regional competitors: they are resourceful, easy to train, and can speak English. Native Filipino skills and talent are further complemented with the training offered by both the academe and the industry's in-house training programs. Hotel and restaurant management courses are offered in many colleges and universities in the Philippines, including the premier universities De La Salle University-College of St. Benilde and the University of the Philippines. More than the academic courses, the hotel and restaurant management courses curriculum in most colleges and universities include practicum wherein students undergo training a local or even foreign hotel establishment (i.e., the College of St. Benilde have their own hotel for student practicum and Perpetual Help College offer training in hotels in Singapore to their top graduates).

Once hired, hotel establishments conduct additional training. New hires undergo on-the-job`training, in the form of apprenticeships, management training programs, and career development seminars. Thus, Filipino hotel and restaurant workers and professionals emerge as among the best in their fields. Indeed, it is not uncommon to find Filipinos (i.e., managers, chefs, waiters, receptionists, and bartenders) working in hotel establishments in the United States, the Middle East, and selected Asian countries.

` Pirating is also a common source of competent hotel workers and professionals among hotel establishments. It is not uncommon for chefs, marketing managers, engineers, and accountants and auditors of a hotel or professional business outfit (i.e., accounting firm) to be offered an incentive (i.e., attractive compensation package) to change employers.

Finally, as most hotels in the country belong to international chains, thus, top management (i.e., general mangers) is commonly composed of foreign nationals sent by the head office. Trained in international hotel operations, foreign managers bring their expertise to the local industry. Foreign expertise is passed down to potential Filipino managers through an understudy program, a condition to foreign national employment.

Industry Training Needs

The Philippines felt the mini-construction boom of hotels and restaurant industries three decades back when Imelda Marcos and Tourism Minister Jose Aspiras launched a tourism campaign that saw the proliferation of deluxe and standard room hotels across town.

This hotel and restaurant management boom paved the way for different schools to give courses in Hotel and Restaurant Management. The first institution to offer training specifically for the hotel and restaurant industry is the Asian Institute of Tourism. Founded on February 26, 1976, the Asian Institute of Tourism is a pioneer in tourism education in the Philippines. Its mission is to upgrade the travel and tourism profession by providing high quality education and training to students who will be the industry's future managers, entrepreneurs and technical experts. The Institute performs the three basic functions of teaching, research and extension, fulfilling the following objectives:

1. to develop entrepreneurs, managers and qualified staff for the tourism industry,
2. to assist in the development, growth and professionalization of tourism,
3. to provide a realistic instructional and research laboratory for tourism operations and management, and
4. to provide a place for the conduct of professional and technical programs for the hospitality industry.

Annex H provides a description of the courses and other services offered by the Asian Institute of Tourism.

AIT's lead was followed by other educational institutions. Examples of schools offering such formal education include De La Salle University (Dasmarinas and the College of St. Benilde), the University of the Philippines, and the International Hotel School, to name a few. Such courses involve basic aspects of hotel operations including the front office, food and beverage, house keeping, and room service, culinary skills, customer care, marketing, accounting, as well as European language skills.

Besides the formal training potential hotel and restaurant workers and professionals receive from the academe, hotel establishments conduct on-the-job training, apprenticeship, management training, and career development seminars (Annex I provides OJT program ratings of selected Hotel and Restaurant Management programs nationwide). A selected few are deployed to training schools managed by the hotels themselves (i.e., Dusit). Technical Education Skills Development Authority (TESDA) also offers training and certification for certain hotel and restaurant industry entry-level positions.

Despite progress made in training hotel and restaurant workers and professionals, resulting in quality personnel, as a continuously evolving industry, a more intensive management training that combine theoretical as well as practical exposure to planning, organizing, staffing, communication, and coping in organizations. Moreover, training programs that strengthen technical skills particularly computer operations, especially with the increasing utilization of information technology in the industry (i.e., reservations, accounting systems, and point-of-sale-system for restaurants) would complement latest "software and hardware" employment.

Deregulation, globalization and radical shifts in leisure and tourism behaviour on the demand side have driven the tourism industry towards information-oriented activities, as seen in the introduction of IT systems in a wide range of spheres in the tourism and leisure sector.

The increasing use of the internet for destination marketing, direct sales and bookings have given rise to electronic tourism markets and at present tourism is among the most important application domains in the World Wide Web. Annex L gives and overall picture of the so-called network economy and the tourism industry. Annex M, on the other hand, illustrates some of the more common technology services and enhancing management information and operation systems multinational hotel companies employ.

Indeed, the internet has brought about some very significant technological changes that enhance its capabilities and viability and its potential to drive electronic commerce. Besides introducing new and innovative business models in both the business-to-business and business-to-consumers markets, the Internet has shortened the value chain and put pressure on all players, especially intermediaries, by giving rise to the so-called "disintermediation" process, that is, the elimination of intermediary organizations such as travel agencies and global distribution systems (GDSs). These intermediary organizations are gradually being replaced by new emerging intermediaries. Annex N depicts the fundamental shifts in the electronic marketplace.

Thus, the challenge for tourism sector players, particularly the small-and medium-sized enterprises (SMEs), is to be able to compete for their market shares and take advantage of emerging opportunities and associated benefits to enhance their profitability and viability in the global marketplace. Annex O sets out the costs and benefits of developing and Internet presence for SMEs. Nonetheless, despite the benefits information technology, particularly electronic data interchange (EDI), can offer SMEs, empirical evidence suggests that SMEs perceive the technology as too complex and cumbersome and that the initial investment is too high. The major obstacles to the introduction of EDI are summarized in Annex P.

Opportunities and Threats

Hotel

Social: Despite the popularity of telephones, faxes, and e-mail, a face-to-face meeting is still the foundation of business relationships. Moreover, businesses generally prefer to hold seminars, workshops, conventions, and training sessions outside their respective companies. Thus, in the years ahead, as science and technology tighten their hold on business and society and the world knits itself ever more tightly into a single market, demand for hotel services is expected to increase.

Travel agents and meeting planners book nearly one out of two hotel rooms, and (the internet notwithstanding) these two groups are still the most frequent intermediaries between the guest and hotel company. They act as information brokers, passing information between guests and managers, process transactions by booking rooms and transferring money, and provide value-added service by integrating their customers' requirements for hotels with other travel needs (i.e., plane tickets and car rentals), while juggling each providers' offering options, constraints, rules and policies.

Thus, travel agents and meeting planners can and do influence a substantial number of bookings. Surprisingly, available data shows that many hotel operators fail to take full advantage of the opportunities presented by intermediaries. Too many hotel operators treat intermediaries as order takers, rather than as partners in pursuit of a common objective – the satisfaction of hotel guest. When hotels make an effort to capture intermediaries' business, the hotels develop for themselves a distinctive position with the intermediaries, and the intermediaries' loyalty appears to go up substantially.

Building the relationship with intermediaries begin with giving the intermediaries access to more precise information on the hotel's brand promises to ensure a correct and satisfactory transaction, as well as providing promotions and incentives and making timely commission payments.

Technology: Large hotels in the country belong to international hotel chains, thus giving local operators access to technological innovations via their parent company. Regular participation in local and overseas trade shows, (i.e., the National Restaurant Show held in McCormick Place, Chicago, the Northern American Association of Food Equipment Manufacturers, and the annual major hotel and restaurant shows held in the Asian region) provide hotel operators with opportunities to update themselves on the latest equipment and IT systems trend in the industry.

Political: The main strength the hotel industry lies in the promotional boost it gets from the tourism programs of the government (i.e., the Centennial Celebration). The Philippine government actively lobbies for the opportunity to host international events. The Miss Universe Pageant and World Expo, for instance encourage tourists to tour the Philippine Islands.

Strong support of industry associations and trade unions (i.e., Hotel and Restaurant Association of the Philippines and the National Union of Workers in the Hotel Restaurant & Allied Industries) enable the hotel industry, among other things, to undertake programs and projects that upgrade and professionalize the sector and to influence government regulatory policies/laws/ rules affecting the industry.

The Philippines is located in the centre of Asia, home of the fastest-growing economies in the world. The archipelago lies southeast of Hong Kong, northeast of Singapore and almost directly north of Kota Kinabalu in Malaysia and Bali, Indonesia. Owing to its accessibility and strategic location, the Philippines is a natural mecca of commerce.

The deregulation of trade in goods and services is expected to enhance the country's natural advantage. Liberalization of trade in services addresses the issue on market access and national treatment. Commitments on the former aim to progressively eliminate restrictions to the entry of foreign services in a country's market while national treatment aim to promote fair treatment between foreign and domestic service providers.

Both hope to reduce uncertainty in the conduct of trade in services. While free movement of capital and labour aim to allow foreign capital and professionals to enter the domestic market. At present, most countries have policies preventing foreign professionals from practicing their profession in the domestic market.

Liberalization is expected to benefit the tourism sector and, therefore, the hotel industry. In particular, deregulating the transport sector, and, thus, allowing new firms to enter the airline and shipping sector will significantly reduce transportation rates, encouraging more a lot of individuals to travel. Likewise, the reduction of tariff rates on hotel equipment, currently at 10%, will allow more hoteliers to either replace or add to their current equipment. Making local establishment more attractive to both local and foreign patrons. Moreover, with liberalization, improvements in technology developed in one country are shared automatically with other countries. They are shared directly when they are embodied in new capital equipment that would relatively be cheaper with the reduction/removal of tariff and non-tariff barriers. As with other industries, the hotel sub-sector would benefit from the availability of cheaper and more modern technology (i.e., hotel systems such as reservations, accounting, etc.).

Finally, liberalization will allow the free movement and employment of international hotel managers, chefs, cooks and other hotel-related professions in the country.

Restaurant

Social: Moreover, the urban population to which restaurants cater is largely made up of young people who have higher disposable incomes and who are more likely to experiment with different cuisine.

Brand loyalty is particularly strong in the fast food sub-sector of the restaurant industry. Jollibee patrons, for example, generally stay loyal to the franchise regardless of price increases.

Demand for dining out is associated with both the ever-expanding options available, and also with the number one reason most consumers use restaurants: they provide a convenient, reasonably priced experience that offers better flavors and taste sensations than consumers can get at home. This has become particularly critical at a time when more and more women are entering the workforce and consequently have less time to prepare meals at home.

Moreover, the Philippine population is youth-oriented. Almost half of the estimated 75 million Filipinos are below 18. And since a large proportion of fast food consumers is between the ages of 16-24, the annual 2.3% population growth rate guarantees market growth for the sub-sector.

Technology: International food chains and franchises facilitate transfer of technology in the local restaurant sub-sector. They provide training of potential employees and employ strict quality control systems.

In terms of availability of technology, the Philippine market is highly competitive with numerous products and brands offered at reasonable prices, and, therefore, allowing restaurant owners the luxury of choosing the type of technology that best suit their operations.

Equipment purchasing decisions depend on the type of end-user. For instance, local single-unit restaurants need inexpensive equipment, so price is the main guiding factor. On the other hand, fine dining restaurants are willing to pay a premium for high quality, durability, after-sales service, costeffectiveness, reputable supplier and fast delivery. Restaurant owners regularly participate in local and international equipment trade fairs, allowing them access to the latest hotel equipment technology.

Economic: Restaurant patrons cross all economic groups. Fast foods and food courts cater to all income classes. Speciality fine dining restaurants, generally target the A, B, and C crowd.

The proliferation of one-stop shopping malls that offer various recreational facilities and amenities is also an important growth factor. The heavy pedestrian traffic that the malls attract means big business for the restaurant industry, particularly the fast food sub-sector.

Moreover, these malls spare the restaurant industry from spending extensive business development studies for their outlets; mall magnates Henry Sy and John Gokongwei Jr. have established formidable track records in building malls.

Finally, Filipino communities abroad are strong basis for the export of local restaurants and fast food technology. The presence of Goldilocks, Jollibee, Max, Red Ribbon, and Barrio Fiesta, among others, in the US, for example, is a result of demand from Filipino migrants longing for a taste for home.

Political: Strong support of industry associations and trade unions (i.e., Hotel and Restaurant Association of the Philippines and the NWHUAI) enable the hotel industry, among other things, to undertake programs and projects that upgrade and professionalize the sector and to influence government regulatory policies/laws/rules affecting the industry.

Threats

Hotel

Social: The patronage of domestic tourists ensures the survival and profitability of most businesses that are dependent upon tourism primarily because domestic tourists outnumber foreign visitors. In the Philippines, 80% of all tourists are domestic travellers; their total spending, tourists who are at least 18 years old, amounts to about PHP57 billion. Nonetheless, very few hotel operators are able to tap into this market for most domestic travellers depend on family and friends to arrange trips and provide lodging.

Technology: Hoteliers indicate several problems that need to be addressed by current local sources of hotel equipment. One is after-sales-service and availability of spare parts. Some distributors, in many instances, are unreliable and do not have an adequate supply of critical spare parts, especially for laundry equipment. When the equipment breaks down, distributors cannot provide repair service to the customer. This requires hotels to outsource laundry services. The phase-out of old models of machinery because of absence of spare parts support presents another serious problem to hotels. Likewise, difficult economic situations raise financing costs to prohibitive levels for many hotel operators. To reduce exposure, banks also restrict financing to their very best clients, thereby limiting technological improvements to selected hoteliers.

Economic: Economic.and political factors contribute to the lackluster performance of the tourism industry in the past two years. Declining disposable income resulting from the Asian currency crisis and political instability resulted in a 3% contraction in tourist arrivals in 1998 and a 1% increase in 1999. Pressure on hotel prices comes from the drive for value for money. Increased operating efficiency obtained through the computerization has helped to reduce costly waste in the supply chain. However, higher labour, raw materials, and utility costs continue to push operating costs up.

New hotel projects which, are actively being pursued are the Wingate Inns and Aston chain, among others, will add to the already overcrowded market. Wingate's franchisor will build one inn every year until 2003. Investment per property is estimated at US$4.5 million. While Aston International's thrust will be in developing resort-type hotels outside Metro Manila. Finally, liberalization would open the market to more foreign hotel and restaurant professionals (i.e., managers, chefs, etc.), thus, posing a real threat to local talent.

Political: Political instability discourages investors and tourists, the lifeblood of the hotel industry. Uprisings in the provinces, kidnappings, and the current scandal involving the president have reduced tourism considerably and resulted in a little bit over 50% hotel occupancy rate.

Delay of the implementation of the "open skies policy" signed into law by President Fidel Ramos (EO 219). The open skies policy seeks to liberalize the airline industry by allowing more foreign airlines access to local routes, which, in turn, bring more tourists into the country.

Restaurant

Social: Although local entrepreneurs own most fine dining restaurants, an overwhelming number of fast food outlets are American franchises. These outlets, therefore, pose serious competition for local franchises. Particularly since tastes and preferences of consumers tend to favour international, especially, fast foods and restaurants.

Technology: A primary limitation of the industry is that the restaurant business involves perishable goods which have to be disposed of at the earliest possible time. Inventory management is key to balancing raw material demand and supply. In terms of equipment, restaurant owners indicate several problems that need to be addressed by current local sources of hotel equipment. One is aftersales-service and availability of spare parts.

Economic: Restaurant patronage/sales are dependent on the levels of economic activity and real income of local residents and tourists. Periods of high inflation reduce the household income as well as the budget for "eating out". Continuing high rate of new entries into the crowded marketplace results in increased competition in all restaurant sub-sectors. Major players have sought to increase market share by a variety of strategies.

In the fast food sector, many operators have offered substantial discounts, particularly in the burgers/chicken sub-sector, led by Jollibee. In the full-service restaurant subsector, the introduction of multi-concept restaurants, improved food quality, quicker service and targeted advertising have been used to make gains in the market.

These strategies allow industry participants to maintain, if not increase, market share but at the expense of thinning margins. The rising costs of imported food ingredients, notwithstanding the current currency crisis, result in increasing production costs. Profit margin erosion can be remedied by either increasing prices of final product/service or cut corners in production or the delivery of service. Either solution may result in a shrinking customer base.

Finally, liberalization will open the door to new international franchises, which can threaten the viability of local ones. Unrestrained transfer of technology can impede the development of local entrepreneurial talent.

Political: Political instability, resulting in economic slowdown, reduces real income as well as the demand for restaurant services.

Action Plan Enhancing Competitiveness

Recommendations

The following recommendations are presented in the context of the country's commitment to enhance the competitiveness of the hotel and restaurant industry. The intent is to enable the sector to compete more effectively in the local and domestic markets and to enhance the marketability of the country's hotel and restaurant industry's manpower in the international market.

The determinants of a subsector's competitiveness would depend on: 1) the level of expertise/competence of local professionals/businesses, 2) the degree of openness of foreign markets and their demand for local expertise, and 3) the degree of openness of the local regulatory framework (i.e. absence or presence of reciprocity provisions).

Sustainable Tourism Development

1. Equally develop domestic tourism. Balance destination development and promotion between international and domestic tourism. Regularly monitor and measure domestic tourism performance.
2. Drafting, implementation and monitoring of programs for the industry following guidelines adopted at the

international, national, regional, and local levels, after consultations with all parties concerned, including the unions representing workers in the industry. Such programs should incorporate the following principles:

- Natural sites should be protected and strict provisions added to prevent pollution and to control the use of energy and natural resources;
- Existing cultural practices in such areas which are helpful to safeguarding the sites should be upheld;
- Eco-tourism should be promoted.

2. Extension of subsidies and loans for the development of tourist facilities.
3. Identify only three or four destinations for international tourism instead of adopting a diversified tourist promotion approach in order to maximize limited tourism development resources.

Legal/Regulatory Environment

1. Implement progressive liberalization in the airline industry and conclude more bilateral and multilateral agreements to expand its coverage.
2. Study possible legislation that would make liberal exemptions to the Constitutional provision on the practice of foreign professionals in the country.
3. Review bilateral agreements on reciprocal recognition of professionals that may have inconsistencies with the general obligations of GATS.
4. Adopt the recommendations of the review of the labour market test of the Philippines.
5. Pursue ongoing negotiations for mutual recognition agreements with selected countries in the field of accountancy, and use it as a model for negotiations in other professions. In the process of negotiating MRAs, the goals and nature of the MRA should be clearly explained to all parties concerned. Moreover, representatives of accredited professional/industrial organizations should

be directly involved in the negotiations since they are most knowledgeable about their respective professions and industries.

6. In the process of negotiations for a Mutual Recognition Agreement, (1) clearly explain the goals and nature of the MRA to all concerned parties, (2) pursue bilateral arrangements since they are more feasible compared to multilateral negotiations, and (3) solicit the inputs of, and actively involve, accredited professional/industrial organizations in the negotiations.
7. Consolidate the proposals of all business services sectors, and provide for a general framework of action towards a Philippine position in the GATS services negotiations.

System of Incentives

1. Grant system of incentives for renovation
2. Grant tax exemptions to companies that provide training for their employees. This will promote the concept of human resource development as a strategic option in enhancing organizational competitiveness.
3. Allow tax-free and duty-free importation of needed equipment, and tax credits on locally purchased equipment, for capital-intensive business service industries such as rental/leasing of transport equipment, rental/leasing of other equipment, printing and publishing, photographic services, technical testing and analysis, computer related services.
4. Grant income tax holidays to upstart firms.

Human Resource Development

1. Align college curricula with the needs of the industry.
2. Formulate a unifying framework for human resources development that will enable government to determine priority areas in the implementation of training programs to enhance the professional and technical skills of Filipino workers. This unifying framework should provide a better perspective in dealing with issues on globalization,

technological developments, and the quality of education as they affect the level of competitiveness of the country's labour force.

The Canadian Framework, for example, identifies nine key policy requirements for a successful travel and tourism HRD strategy:

a. Industry/Employer Commitment through adequate investment in HRD programs, participation in training strategies, support in student work placements, and serving industry/education advisory committees.

b. Government commitment, particularly in facilitating the coordination efforts between education agencies and the industry in developing an internationally competitive workforce.

c. Incentives in the form of career advancement, improved salary and benefits, and employer contributions.

d. Coordinating Agency, creation of a tourism education council that play a coordinating role for the national and regional development of travel and tourism HRD.

e. Education and Training Standards promote greater work satisfaction, improved chances for advancement, mobility throughout the industry, increased proficiency for a given occupation, and greater job security.

f. Theoretical and Applied Learning, successful tourism economies build partnerships with their university and college systems to provide both applied and theoretical learning opportunities for their workforce.

g. Access and Flexibility, credit transferability must be established between high school, certificate, diploma and degrees, thus providing accessibility to youth, minorities, women and working adults.

h. Partnerships, industry, government and educator involvement on HRD planning needs to be sustainable and not fragmented. Industry can contribute to HRD planning by identifying issues and priorities, and by supporting research into HRD issues, education and training policy for tourism, and labour market trends for tourism.

i. Effective and coordinated marketing and communication strategies by government and industry leaders are needed to advance the understanding of the value of HRD, both in terms of the potential career seeker as well as the industry itself.

3. Strengthen the capability of educational institutions to satisfy industry's need for professionals, particularly in areas where there is a lack of supply.
4. Strengthen the basic education system to enable elementary & secondary schools to equip students the basic skills, primarily the 4Rs (reading, writing, arithmetic, and right conduct). This also includes a strong foundation in the use of English.
5. Conduct a closer study on the human resources development efforts of local firms to pinpoint specific areas of deficiencies.
6. Promote continuing education to enhance the skills of professionals and technical workers to make them more competitive abroad and less vulnerable to displacement by foreigners who enter the local market.
7. Encourage the training and certification (i.e., from the Technical Education and Skills Development Agency) of basic entry-level positions in the hotel and restaurant industry.

Network and Linkages

1. Develop and strengthen linkage among industry players. This will assure industry players a stronger voice when dealing with government regarding the formulation of national policies concerning their respective industries. This will also open up opportunities in terms of pooling of resources, exchange of information, and the conduct of training for members. Industry

associations should also take an active role in the process of negotiating mutual recognition agreements (MRAs) because they are the one who are most familiar with their members' needs, capabilities, and preparedness to face liberalization.

2. Develop and strengthen linkage between industry and academe. This could be done through on-the-job training (OJT) or apprenticeship agreements that would enhance the skills of college students through hands-on training and exposure to the actual workplace. The parties could also come up with consultancy arrangements that would enable firms to benefit from the research capabilities of the faculty of schools, and that would enable academe to tap the expertise of professionals in their academic programs. Finally, industry and academe could institutionalize systems for the continuing education of company personnel either through graduate studies or through in-house training/customized programs that could be provided by schools to the firms.
3. Develop linkages between industry and intermediate industries (i.e., booking and travel agents). Travel agents and meeting planners can and do influence a substantial number of bookings. Building these relationship with intermediaries begin with giving the them access to more precise information on the hotel's brand promises to ensure a correct and satisfactory transaction, as well as providing promotions and incentives and making timely commission payments.
4. Develop and strengthen linkage between industry and government. The industry associations should work closely with government agencies in the following areas: (1) negotiation of MRAs with other countries, (2) review of licensing and regulatory requirements to make them more attuned to present-day requirements, (3) provision and exchange of information regarding both the local and foreign markets, (4) formulation of a national policy for certain industries, (5) provision of continuing education,

(6) marketing efforts abroad, and (7) promotion among their members of various financing sources offered by government, among others. A model that could be closely examined concerning government and industry coordination is the Packaging Centre of the Philippines, one of the flagship projects of the Department of Science and Technology (DOST). It has an Advisory Committee tasked to provide direction and recommendations on its overall program strategy, taking into consideration the inputs of various sectors who have a stake in the packaging industry. This Committee is composed of representatives from the Department of Science and Technology (DOST), Industrial Technology Development Institute (ITDI), Packaging Institute of the Philippines (PIP), PhilExport, NEDA, CHED, and DTI.

5. Develop and strengthen linkage between industry and international associations. Local industry associations should affiliate with international associations, and strengthen their relationships with their counterpart associations in other countries. This will open up opportunities for possible joint venture partnerships and exchange of technology. This might also facilitate discussions regarding the possibility of negotiating mutual recognition agreements.

Joint Ventures/Alliances/Mergers

1. Encourage more local firms and foreign firms to form joint venture partnerships and to explore mutually beneficial arrangements, using the Philippines as base of operations. While local firms will benefit in terms of additional capital investments and the transfer of technology into the country, foreign firms will also derive gains in terms of getting a foothold in the domestic market, and in terms of utilizing their local counterparts' strong understanding of the local business conditions.
2. Encourage the smaller local players to consider the possibility of merging with each other to enable them to build up their capital base and to attain economies of scale

needed to compete effectively in a more competitive environment.

Financing

1. Encourage banks to create special financing schemes to help small-and medium-scale hotel and restaurant firms gain access to more capital needed for investment in advanced technology, and to help them bridge working capital requirements.
2. Encourage banks (e.g. Development Bank of the Philippines) and other financing institutions to provide funds for training and development of local manpower, particularly for small-and medium-scale firms.
3. Provide direct government assistance to professional associations
4. Encourage local business services players to avail of the benefits of the "Productivity Incentive Act"
5. Simplify requirements for availing of loans to encourage firms, particularly the smaller players, to take advantage of financing schemes.
6. Encourage local investors, particularly in closely-linked industries, to pool venture capital funds.
7. Encourage foreign investors to establish commercial presence in certain areas that need expertise and advanced technology (e.g. R&D services).

2

Financial Statements and Auditing in Hospitality Sector

Balance Sheet

In financial accounting, a balance sheet or statement of financial position is a summary of the financial balances of a sole proprietorship, a business partnership or a company. Assets, liabilities and ownership equity are listed as of a specific date, such as the end of its financial year. A balance sheet is often described as a "snapshot of a company's financial condition". Of the four basic financial statements, the balance sheet is the only statement which applies to a single point in time.

A standard company balance sheet has three parts: assets, liabilities and ownership equity. The main categories of assets are usually listed first, and typically in order of liquidity. Assets are followed by the liabilities. The difference between the assets and the liabilities is known as equity or the net assets or the net worth or capital of the company and according to the accounting equation, net worth must equal assets minus liabilities.

Another way to look at the same equation is that assets equals liabilities plus owner's equity. Looking at the equation in this way shows how assets were financed: either by borrowing money (liability) or by using the owner's money (owner's equity). Balance sheets are usually presented with assets in one section and liabilities and net worth in the other section with the two sections "balancing."

Records of the values of each account or line in the balance sheet are usually maintained using a system of accounting known as the double-entry bookkeeping system. A business operating entirely in cash can measure its profits by withdrawing the entire bank balance at the end of the period, plus any cash in hand.

However, many businesses are not paid immediately; they build up inventories of goods and they acquire buildings and equipment.

In other words: businesses have assets and so they can not, even if they want to, immediately turn these into cash at the end of each period. Often, these businesses owe money to suppliers and to tax authorities, and the proprietors do not withdraw all their original capital and profits at the end of each period. In other words businesses also have liabilities.

Origin

It was the Flemish mathematician Simon Stevin who persuaded merchants to make it a rule to summarize accounts at the end of every year in a chapter entitled *Coopmànsbouckhouding op de Italiaensche wyse* (Dutch: "Commercial Book-keeping in the Italian Way") of his *Wisconstigheg hedachtenissen* (Dutch: "Mathematical memoirs", Leiden, 1605–08).

Although the balance sheet he required every enterprise to prepare every year was based on entries of the ledger, it was prepared separately from the major books of account. The oldest semi-public balance sheet recorded was that of the East India Company dated 30 April 1671, which was submitted to the company's General Meeting on in 30 August 1671. The publication and audit of the balance sheet was still a rarity in England until the passing of the Bank Charter Act 1844.

Types

A balance sheet summarizes an organization or individual's assets, equity and liabilities at a specific point in time. Individuals and small businesses tend to have simple balance sheets. Larger businesses tend to have more complex balance sheets, and these are presented in the organization's annual report. Large businesses also may prepare balance sheets for segments of their businesses. A balance sheet is often presented alongside one for a different point in time (typically the previous year) for comparison.

Personal Balance Sheet

A personal balance sheet lists current assets such as cash in checking accounts and savings accounts, long-term assets such as common stock and real estate, current liabilities such as loan debt and mortgage debt due, or overdue, long-term liabilities such as mortgage and other loan debt.

Securities and real estate values are listed at market value rather than at historical cost or cost basis. Personal net worth is the difference between an individual's total assets and total liabilities.

US Small Business Balance Sheet

Sample Small Business Balance Sheet

Assets		*Liabilities and Owners' Equity*	
Cash	$6,600	Liabilities	
Accounts Receivable	$6,200	Notes Payable	$30,000
		Accounts Payable	
		Total liabilities	$30,000
Tools and equipment	$25,000	Owners' equity	
		Capital Stock	$7,000
		Retained Earnings	$800
		Total owners' equity	$7,800
Total	$37,800	*Total*	$37,800

A really small business balance sheet lists current assets such as cash, accounts receivable, and inventory, fixed assets such as land, buildings, and equipment, intangible assets such as patents, and liabilities such as accounts payable, accrued expenses, and long-term debt.

Contingent liabilities such as warranties are noted in the footnotes to the balance sheet. The small business's equity is the difference between total assets and total liabilities.

Public Business Entities Balance Sheet Structure

Guidelines for balance sheets of public business entities are given by the International Accounting Standards Committee and numerous country-specific organizations.

Balance sheet account names and usage depend on the organization's country and the type of organization. Government organizations do not generally follow standards established for individuals or businesses.

If applicable to the business, summary values for the following items should be included on the balance sheet:

Assets

Current assets;

1. Cash and cash equivalents
2. Inventories
3. Accounts receivable
4. Prepaid expenses for future services that will be used within a year.

Fixed assets;

1. Property, plant and equipment
2. Investment property, such as real estate held for investment purposes
3. Intangible assets
4. Financial assets (excluding investments accounted for using the equity method, accounts receivables, and cash and cash equivalents)
5. Investments accounted for using the equity method
6. Biological assets, which are living plants or animals. Bearer biological assets are plants or animals which bear agricultural produce for harvest, such as apple trees grown to produce apples and sheep raised to produce wool.

Liabilities;

1. Accounts payable

2. Provisions for warranties or court decisions
3. Financial liabilities (excluding provisions and accounts payable), such as promissory notes and corporate bonds
4. Liabilities and assets for current tax
5. Deferred tax liabilities and deferred tax assets
6. Minority interest in equity
7. Issued capital and reserves attributable to equity holders of the Parent company
8. Unearned revenue for services paid for by customers but not yet provided.

Equity

The net assets shown by the balance sheet equals the third part of the balance sheet, which is known as the shareholders' equity. Formally, shareholders' equity is part of the company's liabilities: they are funds "owing" to shareholders (after payment of all other liabilities); usually, however, "liabilities" is used in the more restrictive sense of liabilities excluding shareholders' equity. The balance of assets and liabilities (including shareholders' equity) is not a coincidence. Records of the values of each account in the balance sheet are maintained using a system of accounting known as double-entry bookkeeping. In this sense, shareholders' equity by construction must equal assets minus liabilities, and are a residual.

1. Numbers of shares authorized, issued and fully paid, and issued but not fully paid
2. Par value of shares
3. Reconciliation of shares outstanding at the beginning and the end of the period
4. Description of rights, preferences, and restrictions of shares
5. Treasury shares, including shares held by subsidiaries and associates
6. Shares reserved for issuance under options and contracts
7. A description of the nature and purpose of each reserve within owners' equity.

Sample Balance Sheet Structure

The following balance sheet structure is just an example. It does not show all possible kinds of assets, equity and liabilities, but it shows the most usual ones. Because it shows goodwill, it could be a consolidated balance sheet. Monetary values are not shown, summary (total) rows are missing as well.

Income Statement

Income statement, also referred as *profit and loss statement (P&L), earnings statement, operating statement* or *statement of operations,* is a company's financial statement that indicates how the revenue (money received from the sale of products and services before expenses are taken out, also known as the "top line") is transformed into the net income (the result after all revenues and expenses have been accounted for, also known as the "bottom line"). It displays the revenues recognized for a specific period, and the cost and expenses charged against these revenues, including write-offs (e.g., depreciation and amortization of various assets) and taxes. The purpose of the income statement is to show managers and investors whether the company made or lost money during the period being reported.

The important thing to remember about an income statement is that it represents a period of time. This contrasts with the balance sheet, which represents a single moment in time. Charitable organizations that are required to publish financial statements do not produce an income statement. Instead, they produce a similar statement that reflects funding sources compared against program expenses, administrative costs, and other operating commitments.

This statement is commonly referred to as the statement of activities. Revenues and expenses are further categorized in the statement of activities by the donor restrictions on the funds received and expended.

The income statement can be prepared in one of two methods. The Single Step income statement takes a simpler approach, totaling revenues and subtracting expenses to find the bottom line. The more complex Multi-Step income statement (as the name implies) takes several steps to find the bottom line, starting with the gross profit. It then calculates operating expenses and, when deducted from the gross profit, yields income from operations. Adding to income from operations is the difference of other revenues and other expenses. When combined with income from operations, this yields income before taxes. The final step is to deduct taxes, which finally produces the net income for the period measured.

Usefulness and Limitations of Income Statement

Income statements should help investors and creditors determine the past financial performance of the enterprise, predict future performance, and assess the capability of generating future cash flows through report of the income and expenses. However, information of an income statement has several limitations:

- Items that might be relevant but cannot be reliably measured are not reported (*e.g.* brand recognition and loyalty).
- Some numbers depend on accounting methods used (*e.g.* using FIFO or LIFO accounting to measure inventory level).
- Some numbers depend on judgments and estimates (*e.g.* depreciation expense depends on estimated useful life and salvage value).

Income Statement Bond LLC

For the year ended DECEMBER 31 2007:

	$ Debit	$ Credit
Revenues		
GROSS PROFIT (including rental income)		496,397
Expenses:		
Advertising	6,300	
Bank & credit card fees	144	
Bookkeeping	3,350	
Employees	88,000	

Entertainment	5,550
Insurance	750
Legal & professional services	1,575
Licenses	632
Printing, postage & stationery	320
Rent	13,000
Rental mortgages and fees	74,400
Telephone	1,000
Utilities	491
Total expenses	(195,512)
Net income	300,885

Items on Income Statement

Operating Section

- Revenue-Cash inflows or other enhancements of assets of an entity during a period from delivering or producing goods, rendering services, or other activities that constitute the entity's ongoing major operations. It is usually presented as sales minus sales discounts, returns, and allowances.
- Expenses-Cash outflows or other using-up of assets or incurrence of liabilities during a period from delivering or producing goods, rendering services, or carrying out other activities that constitute the entity's ongoing major operations.
  - o General and administrative expenses (G & A)-represent expenses to manage the business (officer salaries, legal and professional fees, utilities, insurance, depreciation of office building and equipment, office rents, office supplies)
  - o Selling expenses-represent expenses needed to sell products (*e.g.*, sales salaries, commissions and travel expenses, advertising, freight, shipping, depreciation of sales store buildings and equipment)

- o Selling General and Administrative expenses (SG&A or SGA)-consist of the combined payroll costs (salaries, commissions, and travel expenses of executives, sales people and employees), and advertising expenses a company incurs. SGA is usually understood as a major portion of non-production related costs, opposing production related costs such as raw material and (direct) labour
- o R & D expenses-represent expenses included in research and development
- o Depreciation-is the charge for a specific period (*i.e.* year, accounting period) with respect to fixed assets that have been capitalised on the balance sheet.

Non-operating Section

- Other revenues or gains-revenues and gains from other than primary business activities (e.g. rent, patents). It also includes unusual gains and losses that are either unusual or infrequent, but not both (e.g. sale of securities or fixed assets)
- Other expenses or losses-expenses or losses not related to primary business operations.

Irregular Items

They are reported separately because this way users can better predict future cash flows-irregular items most likely will not recur. These are reported net of taxes.

- Discontinued operations is the most common type of irregular items. Shifting business location, stopping production temporarily, or changes due to technological improvement do not qualify as discontinued operations.
- Extraordinary items are both unusual (abnormal) and infrequent, for example, unexpected natural disaster, expropriation, prohibitions under new regulations. Note: natural disaster might not qualify depending on location

(e.g. frost damage would not qualify in Canada but would in the tropics).

- Changes in accounting principle is, for example, deciding tc depreciate an investment property that has previously not been depreciated. However, changes in estimates (e.g. estimated useful life of a fixed asset) do not qualify.

Earnings Per Share

Because of its importance, earnings per share (EPS) are required to be disclosed on the face of the income statement. A company which reports any of the irregular items must also report EPS for these items either in the statement or in the notes.

There are two forms of EPS reported:

- Basic: in this case "weighted average of shares outstanding" includes only actual stocks outstanding.
- Diluted: in this case "weighted average of shares outstanding" is calculated as if all stock options, warrants, convertible bonds, and other securities that could be transformed into shares *are* transformed. This increases the number of shares and so EPS decreases. Diluted EPS is considered to be a more reliable way to measure EPS.

Family Fitness and Fun

Statements of Income

Revenues	$12,580.2	$ 10,900.4	$ 8,290.3
Cost of sales	6,740.2	5,650.1	4,524.2
Gross profit	6,835.0	5,657.3	3,270.1
Selling, general and administrative expenses	3,624.6	3,296.3	3,034.0
Other (income) expense, net	1,100.3	(20.0)	18.0
Operating profit	2,122.1	2,166.0	2,013.1
Interest expense, net	119.7	124.1	142.8
Income before income taxes	2,102.4	1,980.9	1,870.3
Provision for income taxes	680.3	620.6	582.0
Net income $ 1,720.1 $ 1,421.3 $ 1,190.3			

Viacom Inc. And Subsidiaries

Consolidated Statements of Operations

			(In millions)
Year Ended December 31,	*2004*	*2003*	*2002*
Revenues	$ 22,525.9	$ 20,827.6	$19,186.8
Expenses:			
Operating	12,545.8	11,879.8	10,735.5
Selling, general and administrative	4,142.1	3,732.3	3,498.6
Depreciation and amortization	809.9	741.9	711.8
Impairment charge (Note 3)	17,997.1	—	—
Total expenses	35,494.9	16,354.0	14,945.9
Operating income (loss)	(12,969.0)	4,473.6	4,240.9
Interest expense	(718.9)	(742.9)	(799.1)
Interest income	25.3	11.7	12.0
Other items, net	7.6	(3.0)	(32.9)
Earnings (loss) from continuing operations before income taxes, equity in earnings (loss) of affiliated companies and minority interest	(13,655.0)	3,739.4	3,420.9
Provision for income taxes	(1,378.6)	(1,497.0)	(1,338.3)
Equity in earnings (loss) of affiliated companies, net of tax	(20.8)	.1	(37.3)
Minority interest, net of tax	(5.1)	(4.7)	(3.3)
Net Income (loss) from continuing operations	(15,059.5)	2,237.8	2,042.0
Discontinued operations (Note 2):			
Earnings (loss) from discontinued operations	(1,182.7)	(718.8)	255.3
Income taxes, net of minority interest	92.4	(83.6)	(90.7)
Net Income (loss) from discontinued operations	(1,090.3)	(802.4)	164.6
Net Income (loss) before cumulative effect of accounting change	(16,149.8)	1,435.4	2,206.6

Cumulative effect of accounting change, net of minority interest and tax (Note 1)	(1,312.4)	(18.5)	(1,480.9)
Net Income (loss)	$ (17,462.2)	$ 1,416.9	$ 725.7

Bottom Line

"Bottom line" is the net income that is calculated after subtracting the expenses from revenue. Since this forms the last line of the income statement, it is informally called "bottom line." It is important to investors as it represents the profit for the year attributable to the shareholders.

Cash Flow Statement

In financial accounting, a cash flow statement, also known as *statement of cash flows* or *funds flow statement*, is a financial statement that shows how changes in balance sheet accounts and income affect cash and cash equivalents, and breaks the analysis down to operating, investing, and financing activities. Essentially, the cash flow statement is concerned with the flow of cash in and cash out of the business. The statement captures both the current operating results and the accompanying changes in the balance sheet. As an analytical tool, the statement of cash flows is useful in determining the short-term viability of a company, particularly its ability to pay bills. International Accounting Standard 7 (IAS 7), is the International Accounting Standard that deals with cash flow statements.

People and groups interested in cash flow statements include:

- Accounting personnel, who need to know whether the organization will be able to cover payroll and other immediate expenses
- Potential lenders or creditors, who want a clear picture of a company's ability to repay
- Potential investors, who need to judge whether the company is financially sound
- Potential employees or contractors, who need to know whether the company will be able to afford compensation
- Shareholders of the business.

Purpose

The cash flow statement was previously known as the flow of funds statement. The cash flow statement reflects a firm's liquidity.

The balance sheet is a snapshot of a firm's financial resources and obligations at a single point in time, and the income statement summarizes a firm's financial transactions over an interval of time. These two financial statements reflect the accrual basis accounting used by firms to match revenues with the expenses associated with generating those revenues.

The cash flow statement includes only inflows and outflows of cash and cash equivalents; it excludes transactions that do not directly affect cash receipts and payments. These noncash transactions include depreciation or write-offs on bad debts or credit losses to name a few. The cash flow statement is a cash basis report on three types of financial activities: operating activities, investing activities, and financing activities. Noncash activities are usually reported in footnotes.

The cash flow statement is intended to

1. provide information on a firm's liquidity and solvency and its ability to change cash flows in future circumstances
2. provide additional information for evaluating changes in assets, liabilities and equity
3. improve the comparability of different firms' operating performance by eliminating the effects of different accounting methods
4. indicate the amount, timing and probability of future cash flows.

The cash flow statement has been adopted as a standard financial statement because it eliminates allocations, which might be derived from different accounting methods, such as various timeframes for depreciating fixed assets.

History and Variations

Cash basis financial statements were common before accrual

basis financial statements. The "flow of funds" statements of the past were cash flow statements.

In 1863, the Dowlais Iron Company had receovered from a business slump, but had no cash to invest for a new blast furnace, despite having made a profit. To explain why there were no funds to invest, the manager made a new financial statement that was called a *comparison balance sheet,* which showed that the company was holding too much inventory. This new financial statement was the genesis of Cash Flow Statement that is used today.

In the United States in 1971, the Financial Accounting Standards Board (FASB) defined rules that made it mandatory under Generally Accepted Accounting Principles (US GAAP) to report sources and uses of funds, but the definition of "funds" was not clear." Net working capital" might be cash or might be the difference between current assets and current liabilities. From the late 1970 to the mid-1980s, the FASB discussed the usefulness of predicting future cash flows. In 1987, FASB Statement No. 95 (FAS 95) mandated that firms provide cash flow statements. In 1992, the International Accounting Standards Board issued International Accounting Standard 7 (IAS 7), *Cash Flow Statements,* which became effective in 1994, mandating that firms provide cash flow statements. US GAAP and IAS 7 rules for cash flow statements are similar. Differences include:

- IAS 7 requires that the cash flow statement include changes in both cash and cash equivalents. US GAAP permits using cash alone or cash and cash equivalents.
- IAS 7 permits bank borrowings (overdraft) in certain countries to be included in cash equivalents rather than being considered a part of financing activities.
- IAS 7 allows interest paid to be included in operating activities or financing activities. US GAAP requires that interest paid be included in operating activities.
- US GAAP (FAS 95) requires that when the direct method is used to present the operating activities of the cash flow statement, a supplemental schedule must also present a cash flow statement using the indirect method. The IASC

strongly recommends the direct method but allows either method. The IASC considers the indirect method less clear to users of financial statements. Cash flow statements are most commonly prepared using the indirect method, which is not especially useful in projecting future cash flows.

Cash Flow Activities

The cash flow statement is partitioned into three segments, namely: cash flow resulting from operating activities, cash flow resulting from investing activities, and cash flow resulting from financing activities. The money coming into the business is called cash inflow, and money going out from the business is called cash outflow.

Operating Activities

Operating activities include the production, sales and delivery of the company's product as well as collecting payment from its customers. This could include purchasing raw materials, building inventory, advertising, and shipping the product.

Under IAS 7, operating cash flows include:

- Receipts from the sale of goods or services
- Receipts for the sale of loans, debt or equity instruments in a trading portfolio
- Interest received on loans
- Dividends received on equity securities
- Payments to suppliers for goods and services
- Payments to employees or on behalf of employees
- Interest payments (alternatively, this can be reported under financing activities in IAS 7, and US GAAP).

Items which are added back to [or subtracted from, as appropriate] the net income figure (which is found on the Income Statement) to arrive at cash flows from operations generally include:

- Depreciation (loss of tangible asset value over time)

- Deferred tax
- Amortization (loss of intangible asset value over time)
- Any gains or losses associated with the sale of a non-current asset, because associated cash flows do not belong in the operating section. (unrealized gains/losses are also added back from the income statement).

Investing Activities

Examples of Investing activities are

- Purchase of an asset (assets can be land, building, equipment, marketable securities, etc.)
- Loans made to suppliers or customers
- Payments related to mergers and acquisitions.

Financing Activities

Financing activities include the inflow of cash from investors such as banks and shareholders, as well as the outflow of cash to shareholders as dividends as the company generates income. Other activities which impact the long-term liabilities and equity of the company are also listed in the financing activities section of the cash flow statement.

Under IAS 7;

- Proceeds from issuing short-term or long-term debt
- Payments of dividends
- Payments for repurchase of company shares
- Repayment of debt principal, including capital leases
- For non-profit organizations, receipts of donor-restricted cash that is limited to long-term purposes.

Items under the financing activities section include:

- Dividends paid
- Sale or repurchase of the company's stock
- Net borrowings
- Payment of dividend tax.

Disclosure of Noncash Activities

Under IAS 7, noncash investing and financing activities are disclosed in footnotes to the financial statements.

Under US General Accepted Accounting Principles (GAAP), noncash activities may be disclosed in a footnote or within the cash flow statement itself. Noncash financing activities may include

- Leasing to purchase an asset
- Converting debt to equity
- Exchanging noncash assets or liabilities for other noncash assets or liabilities
- Issuing shares in exchange for assets.

Preparation Methods

The direct method of preparing a cash flow statement results in a more easily understood report. The indirect method is almost universally used, because FAS 95 requires a supplementary report similar to the indirect method if a company chooses to use the direct method.

Indirect Method

The indirect method uses net-income as a starting point, makes adjustments for all transactions for non-cash items, then adjusts for all cash-based transactions. An increase in an asset account is subtracted from net income, and an increase in a liability account is added back to net income. This method converts accrual-basis net income (or loss) into cash flow by using a series of additions and deductions.

Direct Method

The direct method for creating a cash flow statement reports major classes of gross cash receipts and payments. Under IAS 7, dividends received may be reported under operating activities or under investing activities.

If taxes paid are directly linked to operating activities, they are reported under operating activities; if the taxes are directly linked to investing activities or financing activities, they are reported under investing or financing activities.

Sample cash flow statement using the direct method :

Cash flows from (used in) operating activities

Cash receipts from customers	27,500
Cash paid to suppliers and employees	(20,000)
Cash generated from operations (sum)	7,500
Interest paid	(2,000)
Income taxes paid	(4,000)
Net cash flows from operating activities	1,500

Cash flows from (used in) investing activities

Proceeds from the sale of equipment	7,500
Dividends received	3,000
Net cash flows from investing activities	10,500
Cash flows from (used in) financing	
activities Dividends paid	(2,500)
Net cash flows used in financing activities	(2,500).
Net increase in cash and cash equivalents	9,500
Cash and cash equivalents, beginning of year	1,000
Cash and cash equivalents, end of year	$10,500

Rules

The following rules are used to make adjustments for changes in current assets and liabilities, operating items not providing or using cash and nonoperating items.

- Likami
- Increase in non-cash current asset are subtracted from net income
- Increase in current liabilities are added to net income
- Decrease in current liabilities are subtracted from net income

- Expenses with no cash outflows are added back to net income (depreciation and/or amortization expense are the only operating items that have no effect on cash flows in the period)
- Revenues with no cash inflows are subtracted from net income
- Non operating losses are added back to net income
- Non operating gains are subtracted from net income.

Example: cash flow of Citigroup:

Citigroup Cash Flow Statement (all numbers in millions of US$)

Period ending	*12/31/2007*	*12/31/2006*	*12/31/2005*
Net income	21,538	24,589	17,046
Operating activities, cash flows provided by or used in:			
Depreciation and amortization	2,790	2,592	2,747
Adjustments to net income	4,617	621	2,910
Decrease (increase) in accounts receivable	12,503	17,236	–
Increase (decrease) in liabilities (A/P, taxes payable)	131,622	19,822	37,856
Decrease (increase) in inventories	–	–	–
Increase (decrease) in other operating activities	(173,057)	(33,061)	(62,963)
Net cash flow from operating activities	13	31,799	(2,404)
Investing activities, cash flows provided by or used in:			
Capital expenditures	(4,035)	(3,724)	(3,011)
Investments	(201,777)	(71,710)	(75,649)
Other cash flows from investing activities	1,606	17,009	(571)
Net cash flows from investing activities	(204,206)	(58,425)	(79,231)

Financing activities, cash flows provided by or used in:			
Dividends paid	(9,826)	(9,188)	(8,375)
Sale (repurchase) of stock	(5,327)	(12,090)	133
Increase (decrease) in debt	101,122	26,651	21,204
Other cash flows from financing activities	120,461	27,910	70,349
Net cash flows from financing activities	206,430	33,283	83,311
Effect of exchange rate changes	645	(1,840)	731
Net increase (decrease) in cash and cash equivalents	2,882	4,817	2,407

Equity (Finance)

In accounting and finance, equity is the residual claim or interest of the most junior class of investors in assets, after all liabilities are paid. If valuations placed on assets do not exceed liabilities, negative equity exists. In an accounting context, Shareholders' equity (or stockholders' equity, shareholders' funds, shareholders' capital or similar terms) represents the remaining interest in assets of a company, spread among individual shareholders of common or preferred stock.

At the start of a business, owners put some funding into the business to finance assets. This creates liability on the business in the shape of capital as the business is a separate entity from its owners. Businesses can be considered to be, for accounting purposes, sums of liabilities and assets; this is the accounting equation. After liabilities have been accounted for, the positive remainder is deemed the owner's interest in the business.

This definition is helpful to understand the liquidation process in case of bankruptcy. At first, all the secured creditors are paid against proceeds from assets. Afterward, a series of creditors, ranked in priority sequence, have the next claim/right on the residual proceeds. Ownership equity is the last or residual claim against assets, paid only after all other creditors are paid. In such cases where even creditors could not get enough money to pay their bills, and nothing is left over to reimburse owners' equity. Thus owners' equity is reduced to zero. Ownership equity is also known as risk capital, liable capital and equity.

Equity Investments

Equity investments generally refers to the buying and holding of shares of stock on a stock market by individuals and firms in anticipation of income from dividends and capital gain as the value of the stock rises. It also sometimes refers to the acquisition of equity (ownership) participation in a private (unlisted) company or a startup (a company being created or newly created). When the investment is in infant companies, it is referred to as venture capital investing and is generally understood to be higher risk than investment in listed going-concern situations.

The equities held by private individuals are often held via mutual funds or other forms of pooled investment vehicle, many of which have quoted prices that are listed in financial newspapers or magazines; the mutual funds are typically managed by prominent fund management firms (e.g. Schroders, Fidelity Investments or the Vanguard Group). Such holdings allow individual investors to obtain the diversification of the fund(s) and to obtain the skill of the professional fund managers in charge of the fund(s). An alternative, usually employed by large private investors and pension funds, is to hold shares directly; in the institutional environment many clients who own portfolios have what are called segregated funds as opposed to, or in addition to, the pooled e.g. mutual fund alternative.

A calculation can be made to assess whether an equity is over or underpriced compared with a long-term government bond. This is called the Yield Gap or Yield Ratio. It is the ratio of the dividend yield of an equity and that of the long-term bond.

Accounting

In financial accounting, it is the owners' interest on the assets of the enterprise after deducting all its liabilities. It appears on the balance sheet/Statement of Financial Position, one of the four primary financial statements.

Ownership equity includes both tangible and intangible items (such as brand names and reputation/goodwill).

Accounts listed under ownership equity include (example):

- Preferred stock
- Share capital, common stock
- Capital surplus
- Stock options
- Retained earnings
- Treasury stock
- Reserve (accounting).

Book Value

The book value of equity will change in the case of the following events:

- Changes in the firm's assets relative to its liabilities. For example, a profitable firm receives more cash for its products than the cost at which it produced these goods, and so in the act of making a profit it is increasing its assets.
- Depreciation. Equity will decrease, for example, when machinery depreciates, which is registered as a decline in the value of the asset, and on the liabilities side of the firm's balance sheet as a decrease in shareholders' equity.
- Issue of new equity in which the firm obtains new capital increases the total shareholders' equity.
- Share repurchases, in which a firm gives back money to its investors, reducing on the asset side its financial assets, and on the liability side the shareholders' equity. For practical purposes (except for its tax consequences), share repurchasing is similar to a dividend payment, as both consist of the firm giving money back to investors. Rather than giving money to all shareholders immediately in the form of a dividend payment, a share repurchase reduces the number of shares (increases the size of each share) in future income and distributions.

- Dividends paid out to preferred stock owners are considered an expense to be subtracted from net income (from the point of view of the common share owners).
- Other reasons. Assets and liabilities can change without any effect being measured in the Income Statement under certain circumstances; for example, changes in accounting rules may be applied retroactively. Sometimes assets bought and held in other countries get translated back into the reporting currency at different exchange rates, resulting in a changed value.

Shareholders' Equity

When the owners are shareholders, the interest can be called shareholders' equity; the accounting remains the same, and it is ownership equity spread out among shareholders. If all shareholders are in one and the same class, they share equally in ownership equity from all perspectives. However, shareholders may allow different priority ranking among themselves by the use of share classes, and options. This complicates both analysis for stock valuation, and accounting.

The individual investor is interested not only in the total changes to equity, but also in the increase/decrease in the value of his own personal share of the equity. This reconciliation of equity should be done both in total and on a per share basis.

- Equity (beg. of year)
- + net income inter net money you gained
- " dividends how much money you gained ŏr lost so far
- +/" gain/loss from changes to the number of shares outstanding.more or less
- = Equity (end of year) if you get more money during the year or less or not anything.

Market Value of Shares

In the stock market, market price per share does not correspond to the equity per share calculated in the accounting statements. Stock valuations, often much higher, are based on other considerations related to the business' operating cashflow, profits and future prospects; some factors are derived from the accounting statements. Thus, there is little or no correlation between the equity seen in financial statements and the stock valuation of the business.

Real Estate Equity

Individuals can also use market valuations to calculate equity in real estate. An owner refers to his or her equity in a property as the difference between the market price of a property and the liability attached to the property (mortgage or home equity loan).

Statement of Retained Earnings

The Statement of Retained Earnings (also known as Equity Statement, Statement of Owner's Equity for a single proprietorship, Statement of Partner's Equity for partnership, and Statement of Retained Earnings and Stockholders' Equity for corporation) is one of the basic financial statements as per Generally Accepted Accounting Principles, and it explains the changes in a company's retained earnings over the reporting period. It breaks down changes affecting the account, such as profits or losses from operations, dividends paid, and any other items charged or credited to retained earnings. A retained earnings statement is required by Generally Accepted Accounting Principles (GAAP) whenever comparative balance sheets and income statements are presented. It may appear in the balance sheet, in a combined income statement and changes in retained earnings statement, or as a separate schedule.

Therefore, the statement of retained earnings uses information from the income statement and provides information to the balance sheet. Retained earnings are part of the balance sheet (another basic financial statement) under "stockholders equity," and is mostly affected by net income earned during a period of time by the company less any dividends paid to the company's owners/ stockholders. The retained earnings account on the balance sheet is said to represent an "accumulation of earnings" since net profits and losses are added/subtracted from the account from period to period.

The general equation can be expressed as following:

Ending Retained Earnings = Beginning Retained Earnings-Dividends Paid + Net Income.

Generally Accepted Auditing Standards

Generally Accepted Auditing Standards, or GAAS are sets of standards against which the quality of audits may be judged. Several organizations have developed such sets of principles, which vary by territory.

US GAAS

US GAAS are ten auditing standards, developed by the American Institute of Certified Public Accountants, consisting of general standards, standards of field work, and standards of reporting, along with interpretations. They were developed by the AICPA in 1947 and have undergone minor changes since then.

The US GAAS are as follows:

General Standards

1. The auditor must have adequate technical training and proficiency to perform the audit.
2. The auditor must maintain independence in mental attitude in all matters related to the audit.
3. The auditor must use due professional care during the performance of the audit and the preparation of the report.

ISAs

International Standards on Auditing are developed by the International Auditing and Assurance Standards Board of the International Federation of Accountants. Derivatives of ISAs are used in the audit of several other juristictions, including the United Kingdom.

Internal Audit

Internal auditing is a profession and activity involved in helping organizations achieve their stated objectives. It does this by using a systematic methodology for analysing business processes, procedures and activities with the goal of highlighting organizational problems and recommending solutions. Professionals called internal auditors are employed by organizations to perform the internal auditing activity.

The scope of internal auditing within an organization is broad and may involve topics such as the efficacy of operations, the reliability of financial reporting, deterring and investigating fraud, safeguarding assets, and compliance with laws and regulations.

Internal auditing frequently involves measuring compliance with the entity's policies and procedures. However, Internal auditors are not responsible for the execution of company activities; they advise management and the Board of Directors (or similar oversight body) regarding how to better execute their responsibilities. As a result of their broad scope of involvement, internal auditors may have a variety of higher educational and professional backgrounds.

Publicly-traded corporations typically have an internal auditing department, led by a Chief Audit Executive ("CAE") who generally reports to the Audit Committee of the Board of Directors, with administrative reporting to the Chief Executive Officer.

The profession is unregulated, though there are a number of international standard setting bodies, an example of which is the Institute of Internal Auditors ("IIA"). The IIA has established Standards for the Professional Practice of Internal Auditing and has over 150,000 members representing 165 countries, including approximately 65,000 Certified Internal Auditors.

History of Internal Auditing

The Internal Auditing profession evolved steadily with the progress of management science after World War II. It is conceptually similar in many ways to financial auditing by public accounting firms, quality assurance and banking compliance activities. Much of the theory underlying internal auditing is derived from management consulting and public accounting professions. With the implementation in the United States of the Sarbanes-Oxley Act of 2002, the profession's growth accelerated, as many internal auditors possess the skills required to help companies meet the requirements of the law.

Organizational Independence

To perform their role effectively, internal auditors require organizational independence from management, to enable unrestricted evaluation of management activities and personnel. Although internal auditors are part of company management and paid by the company, the primary customer of internal audit activity is the entity charged with oversight of management's activities. This is typically the Audit Committee, a subcommittee of the Board of Directors. To provide independence, most Chief Audit Executives report to the Chairperson of the Audit Committee and can only be replaced with the concurrence of that individual.

Role in Internal Control

Internal auditing activity is primarily directed at improving internal control. Under the COSO Framework, internal control is broadly defined as a process, effected by an entity's board of directors, management, and other personnel, designed to provide reasonable assurance regarding the achievement of objectives in the following internal control categories:

- Effectiveness and efficiency of operations.
- Reliability of financial reporting.
- Compliance with laws and regulations.

Management is responsible for internal control. Managers establish policies and processes to help the organization achieve specific objectives in each of these categories. Internal auditors perform audits to evaluate whether the policies and processes are designed and operating effectively and provide recommendations for improvement.

In the United States, internal auditors may assist management with compliance with the Sarbanes-Oxley Act (SOX).

Role in Risk Management

Internal auditing professional standards require the function to monitor and evaluate the effectiveness of the organization's

Risk management processes. Risk management relates to how an organization sets objectives, then identifies, analyses, and responds to those risks that could potentially impact its ability to realize its objectives.

Under the COSO enterprise risk management (ERM) Framework, risks fall under strategic, operational, financial reporting, and legal/regulatory categories. Management performs risk assessment activities as part of the ordinary course of business in each of these categories. Examples include: strategic planning, marketing planning, capital planning, budgeting, hedging, incentive payout structure, and credit/lending practices. Sarbanes-Oxley regulations also require extensive risk assessment of financial reporting processes. Corporate legal counsel often prepares comprehensive assessments of the current and potential litigation a company faces. Internal auditors may evaluate each of these activities, or focus on the processes used by management to report and monitor the risks identified. For example, internal auditors can advise management regarding the reporting of forward-looking operating measures to the Board, to help identify emerging risks.

In larger organizations, major strategic initiatives are implemented to achieve objectives and drive changes. As a member of senior management, the Chief Audit Executive (CAE) may participate in status updates on these major initiatives. This places the CAE in the position to report on many of the major risks the organization faces to the Audit Committee, or ensure management's reporting is effective for that purpose.

Internal auditors may help companies establish and maintain Enterprise Risk Management processes. Internal auditors also play an important role in helping companies execute a SOX 404 top-down risk assessment. In these latter two areas, internal auditors typically are part of the project team in an advisory role.

Role in Corporate Governance

Internal auditing activity as it relates to corporate governance is generally informal, accomplished primarily through participation in meetings and discussions with members of the Board of Directors. Corporate governance is a combination of processes and organizational structures implemented by the Board of Directors to inform, direct, manage, and monitor the organization's resources, strategies and policies towards the achievement of the organizations objectives. The internal auditor is often considered one of the "four pillars" of corporate governance, the other pillars being the Board of Directors, management, and the external auditor.

A primary focus area of internal auditing as it relates to corporate governance is helping the Audit Committee of the Board of Directors (or equivalent) perform its responsibilities effectively. This may include reporting critical internal control problems, informing the Committee privately on the capabilities of key managers, suggesting questions or topics for the Audit Committee's meeting agendas, and coordinating carefully with the external auditor and management to ensure the Committee receives effective information.

Nature of the Internal Audit Activity

Based on a risk assessment of the organization, internal auditors, management and oversight Boards determine where to focus internal auditing efforts. Internal auditing activity is generally conducted as one or more discrete projects. A typical internal audit project involves the following steps:

1. Establish and communicate the scope and objectives for the audit to appropriate management.
2. Develop an understanding of the business area under review. This includes objectives, measurements, and key transaction types. This involves review of documents and interviews. Flowcharts and narratives may be created if necessary.
3. Describe the key risks facing the business activities within the scope of the audit.
4. Identify control procedures used to ensure each key risk and transaction type is properly controlled and monitored.
5. Develop and execute a risk-based sampling and testing approach to determine whether the most important controls are operating as intended.

6. Report problems identified and negotiate action plans with management to address the problems.
7. Follow-up on reported findings at appropriate intervals. Internal audit departments maintain a follow-up database for this purpose.

Project length varies based on the complexity of the activity being audited and Internal Audit resources available. Many of the above steps are iterative and may not all occur in the sequence indicated.

By analysing and recommending business improvements in critical areas, auditors help the organization meet its objectives. In addition to assessing business processes, specialists called Information Technology (IT) Auditors review information technology controls.

Developing the Plan of Engagements

Internal auditing standards require the development of a plan of audit engagements (projects) based on a risk assessment, updated at least annually. The input of senior management and the Board is typically included in this process. Many departments update their plan of engagements throughout the year as risks or organizational priorities change. This effort helps ensure the audit activity is aligned with the organization's objectives, by answering two key questions: First, what goals are the organization trying to accomplish in the upcoming period? Second, how can the Internal Audit Department assist the organization in achieving these goals?

Internal auditors often conduct a series of interviews of senior management to identify potential engagements. Changes in people, processes, or systems often generate audit project ideas. Various documents are reviewed, such as strategic plans, financial reports, consulting studies, etc.

Further, the results of prior audits and resolution of open issues are considered. For example, even if a business area is important, prior audit work and the nature and status of open issues may render further audit effort unnecessary. If the organization has a formal enterprise risk management (ERM) program, the risks identified therein help limit the amount of separate risk assessment performed by Internal Audit.

The preliminary plan of engagements is documented and prioritized. Audit resources and expertise are then considered and a final plan is presented to senior management and the Audit Committee. The presentations vary based on the needs of the stakeholders and may include the following:

- Summary of key goals, risks and corresponding major audits, to illustrate alignment;
- Analyses of audit effort along a variety of dimensions (e.g., by business segment, COSO objective category, IT, Sarbanes-Oxley, vs. prior year, etc.) along with commentary regarding changes;
- Brief description of critical projects identified;
- Projects requested but not planned for execution due to prioritization and resources;
- Required co-sourcing effort, typically where outside expertise is required or during peak periods;
- Coordination with other risk functions, such as legal, compliance or insurance, to ensure coverage of key organizational risks;
- Update on audit staffing levels, experience and certification; and
- Appendix materials, such as planning approach, assumptions (e.g., days per auditor and staffing level) and brief descriptions of all planned audits and related prioritization.

Best Practices in Internal Auditing

Measuring the Internal Audit Function

The measurement of the internal audit function can involve a balanced scorecard approach. Internal audit functions are primarily evaluated based on the quality of counsel and information provided to the Audit Committee and top management. However, this is primarily qualitative and therefore difficult to measure.

"Customer surveys" sent to key managers after each audit project or report can be used to measure performance, with an annual survey to the Audit Committee. Scoring on dimensions such as professionalism, quality of counsel, timeliness of work product, utility of meetings, and quality of status updates are typical with such surveys. Understanding the expectations of senior management and the audit committee represent important steps in developing a performance measurement process, as well as how such measures help align the audit function with organizational priorities.

Quantitative measures can also be used to measure the function's level of execution and qualifications of its personnel. Key measures include:

Plan completion: This is a measure of the degree to which the annual plan of engagements is completed, measured at a point in time. This may be measured using the number of projects completed, weighted by the planned size of each project, with estimates for projects in-progress. Measured throughout the year, it is compared against the percentage of the year elapsed.

Report issuance: This is a measure of the time elapsed from completion of testing to issuance of the final audit report, including management's action plans. This can be measured in average days or percentage of reports issued within a certain standard, such as 30 days. Establishing expectations for the timing of management's response to report recommendations is critical. In addition, the scope and degree of change involved in the report's action plans are key variables. For example, a report for a single retail store requiring only the store manager's action might take 3–5 days to issue. However, a report consolidating findings from 20 retail stores, with action plans with national implications determined by top management, may take 30–60 days in complex organizations.

Issue closure: Reported audit findings are often called "issues" or "deficiencies." Professional standards require audit functions to track reported findings to resolution, which effectively requires the maintenance of an issues follow-up database. The number of days that reported issues remain open, or open after their agreed-upon closure date, are key measures. In addition, reporting database statistics such as the number of issues open (unresolved), closed (resolved), and issues opened/closed during a given period are useful statistics.

Staff qualifications: This can be measured through the percentage of staff with professional certifications, graduate degrees, and overall years of experience.

Staff utilization rate: This is measured as the percentage of time spent on projects, as opposed to administrative time such as training or vacation. Many internal audit departments track time by audit project. This is typically captured in a database or spreadsheet.

Staffing level: The number of positions filled relative to the authorized staffing level. Due to the challenge of finding qualified staff, departments may have rotational programs to bring in management to complete tours in the function or be "guest" auditors. Audit departments also "co-source," meaning they obtain contract auditors from service providers.

Developing and Retaining Staff

Developing and retaining quality professionals is a key concern in the profession. Key methods for developing and retaining internal audit staff personnel include:

- Providing challenging, varied assignments
- Ensuring quality supervision
- Ensuring staff participates in projects from start to finish, to learn all phases of the audit process
- Providing opportunities to lead (in-charge) projects, starting with more structured projects such as Sarbanes-Oxley work
- Participating on departmental improvement task forces, such as preparation for quality assurance review
- Participating in the recruiting and interviewing process for new hires
- Rotating through various audit teams (in larger departments) or audits of various businesses

- Providing both outside training (e.g., seminars) and in-house training (e.g., company systems) for two weeks/ year
- Participation in annual risk assessment activities, whether asking key questions or just taking notes.

Reporting of Critical Findings

The Chief Audit Executive (CAE) typically reports the most critical issues to the Audit Committee quarterly, along with management's progress towards resolving them. Critical issues typically have a reasonable likelihood of causing substantial financial or reputational damage to the company. For particularly complex issues, the responsible manager may participate in the discussion. Such reporting is critical to ensure the function is respected, that the proper "tone at the top" exists in the organization, and to expedite resolution of such issues. It is a matter of considerable judgment to select appropriate issues for the Audit Committee's attention and to describe them in the proper context.

3

Internal and Departmental Accounting

It is a bit difficult to give a precise definition of the word 'audit'. Originally its meaning and use was confined merely to auditing of 'Cash'. These days auditing has a wide usage and it now means a thorough scrutiny of the books of accounts and its ultimate aim is to verify the financial position disclosed by the Trading Account, Profit and Loss Account and Balance Sheet.

Auditing is a systematic examination of the books and records of a business or other organization in order to ascertain or verify and to report upon the facts regarding its financial operation and the result thereof'.

R. B. BOSS has defined as 'Audit may be said to be verification of the accuracy and correctness of the books of accounts by independent person qualified for the job and not in any way connected with the preparation of such accounts'.

Auditing is the verification of the correctness of accounts and reliability of accounting system, data and information. An auditing, therefore, includes verification of correctness of the accounts, statements, reports, data, etc. and finally checking these data to see that they adhere to accounting principles, plans, procedures and objectives.

The origin of auditing is traced back to the 18th century. The need of auditing was felt as the practice of large scale production was developed as a result of industrial revolution.

The word 'audit' is derived from the Latin Word 'auditure' which means to hear. Formerly a person responsible for maintenance of accounts went to some impartial and experienced person, who used to check these accounts and express his opinion about its correctness. These experienced persons were known as 'auditors'.

The aim of the audit department is to assess the accuracy and reliability of accounting system, data, information, and to assess the business efficiency and general operation. Internal auditor is an integral part of the company's internal control system. Though it is optional but all large organization do have internal auditing.

Role of the Auditor

The role of the internal auditor normally involves checking, verifying and reporting on:

1. Financial information required by the management.
2. Costing information required by the management for example budget, variances, cash forecasting, etc.
3. Effectiveness of internal control system, preventing loss of assets or manipulation of accounting data.
4. Efficiency of companies management particularly in the way in which it formulates its plans, policies and decisions.

Auditing in India

The Chartered Accountants Act was passed in 1949 and it came in existence from July 1, 1949. The regulation control and management of the profession passed from the Central Government to the profession i.e. in the hands of the Institute of Chartered Accountants of India which was formed by the Act of Parliament. Now a person has to pass the examination conducted by the Institute of Chartered Accountant to obtain a degree of Chartered Accountant and gets a license to practice as a chartered accountant.

Internal Auditor

A person or a group of persons deputed to audit the accounts is/are called Internal Auditor/s. These persons may be an internal part of the organization (employees) or can be hired from outside agency to audit the accounts. Internal auditing of accounts *is* not compulsory. The Internal Auditor may not be registered Chartered Accountant (C.A.).

Duties of Auditor

The most important duties of internal auditors are as follows

1. Internal auditor checks all the vouchers and ensures their correctness. He goes through the procedures and methods of accounting adopted by the management. He audits all the assets and liabilities like machinery, equipment, capital, reserve, etc. and he also audits the incomes and expenditure accounts.
2. He ensures that accounting records are kept accurately and according to the schedules.
3. He detects all kind of errors and protects the company from frauds.
4. He checks the prescribed control plans and if these require modification than suggests the remedial measures.
5. He checks the non accounting areas such as administration, marketing, securities, etc. and suggests the better control measurements.
6. He checks and submits his report on budgets,' variances, cash forecasts, sales forecasts, food cost forecasts, labour cost forecasts, etc.
7. He debits all rooms with room charges at 12 midnight before closing the accounts for the day.

The internal auditor, by virtue of his duties and responsibilities is an integral part of the organisation's internal control system.

Advantages of Auditing

An auditing is not only useful to the management but it also ensures socioeconomic benefits.

The following are the advantages of auditing:

Benefits to the Management

1. It detects the errors and frauds.
2. It keeps employees more alert.
3. It reduces the wear and tear of assets and also helps in better utilization of assets.
4. It increases profitability.
5. It reduces the cost due to better management, efficiency and control.
6. It points out management's weakness and recommends better accounting systems.

Benefits to Share Holders and General Public

1. This tells the public whether it is making sufficient profits or not.
2. In its reports, it gives the information like earning per share, cash earning per share, debt equity ratio, price equity ratio, comparative balance sheets, comparative income expenditure statements, etc. This helps public and share holders in deciding whether to invest in the company or not.
3. The public gets goods and services at reasonable prices.

Benefits to the Government

1. The bills at cost plus profit submitted to the government are settled without dispute.
2. The government can fix prices of essential commodities.
3. The subsidies can be decided after studying the cost and selling price government wants to fix.
4. It helps in fixing the export price for commodities.
5. The income tax and other tax authorities accept the reports submitted by the auditors.

Though auditing has many advantages but the effectiveness of this department depends on the following limitations

1. *Qualification :* The auditors must be well qualified and they must know their job perfectly.

2. *Experience* : The prior experience of auditing is very essential to audit the accounts accurately.
3. *Independence* : The auditors must be extended independence. That is why usually they are hired from outside. Even if internal auditor/employee are to be used then he must not work under accounts department. In fact he should report to General Manager or Director of the company.
4. *Access to Records* :The auditors must have an authority to have any or all the documents, files, etc. for the purpose of auditing.
5. *Safety* :The auditors must not feel unsafe for submitting adverse reports on the organisation in general or any department in particular.
6. *Adequate Staff* :There should be adequate number of persons to carry out the work.

Limitations of Internal Audit

An Internal Auditing is an expensive affair and the small organizations do not find it viable to have their accounts audited internally. But the larger companies find it very essential to have internal auditors. It helps in improving the financial position and cost efficiency of the business.

Summary

Internal auditing is a part of internal control system. !t is a perpetual verification of accounting books, bills, vouchers, cash receipts, payments, bank reconciliation, utmost utilization of assets, safety and control of assets, control of bad debts, etc. They are responsible for accounting procedure, finding budget variances, ensuring organisation principles, policies, etc. It is possible either its organization can have its own employees or appoint an outside agency to perform the duties of internal auditing. Small organizations generally do not have separate audit department nor arrange any outside agency. Internal auditor will head the department and report to General Manager/Chief Accountant/ Director.

External Audit/Statutory Audit

It is a compulsory audit done by outside agency at least once, at the end of the financial year. As per SERI guidelines public limited companies are required to have the companies accounts audited after every three months. Only registered Chartered Accountant Auditors are authorised to audit the accounts and sign it. The following are the reasons to have statutory auditing;

1. All Public Limited Companies must have their accounts audited by external auditors.
2. All Government departments and Government owned companies must get their accounts audited from external Government approved auditors (usually A.G. Office).
3. All Government funded organisations, societies; corporations must get their accounts audited.
4. All registered societies, which collect donations from public, must get their accounts audited from external auditors.
5. Any company which intends to borrow money from government or financial institutions must get their accounts audited.
6. Any other company may be asked to get their accounts audited from external auditors.

Auditing conducted according to statutes is called 'Statutory Audit'.

The Statutory Auditor starts his work by studying the nature of the business and its organization, the books of accounts maintained, the procedure in use, the principles of accounting systems adopted and the nature and extent of the various internal checks and control exercised.

The auditors follow the following procedure for auditing the accounts

1. He checks all the vouchers and ensures its correctness from the documents attached.
2. He checks the arithmetical accuracy of the bills, vouchers,

reports, records, etc. The totals of each page, carried forward, brought forward, etc. are also checked. He puts a tick mark for every transaction checked.

3. He must ensure that no over payments or wrong payments are made and all norms for purchases have been followed.
4. He must check the rules and regulations, powers and authorities of each officer and must ensure that all rules are followed.
5. All cuttings must be signed by authorised persons.
6. Audit reports must be submitted along with objections/ notes etc. All the objections must be rectified.

Audit for Hotels

The auditing for hotels differs from the type, size of the hotel. The degree of mechanization has a great impact on the auditing of a hotel. The auditor must examine the system or internal check in vogue with regard to the ordering, purchases, receiving, storing, storing, issuing, etc. He is also expected to check the system of book and record keeping in vogue in the hotel. The cash books receipt and payment side must be checked and tallied with check books. Ali cuttings, overwriting, discounts, allowances, missing checks, etc. must be examined. All receipts must be made against the proper printed and signed receipts and should be entered either in the sales summary sheets or cash book.

As far as possible no cash payments should be made expect payments made by petty cashier. Salaries and wages must be paid by cheques after receiving the bills from personnel department and attendance from Time Office and the concerned departments. Cheques should be issued to suppliers against their bills along with the supply order, invoice, store keeper's receipt, etc.).

Night Auditing in Hotels

Each hotel appoints a night auditor who works independently and reports to either Chief Accountant or to General Manager. His duty starts after 9 p.m. and works until next day morning. Due to his night working hours he is termed as Night Auditor. He audits the accounts of Front Office Cashiers. He performs the following duties;

1. Reconcile all sales statements submitted by the various departments cashiers to front office cashiers throughout the day.
2. He verifies all the debit and credit vouchers at Front Office Cash. 3. Checks guest folios.
4. Verifies Front Office Cashiers Report.
5. In some hotels he is also required to post the un posted vouchers at Front Desk and also debit all rooms with the day's room tariff.
6. In case of Cash Register Machine (like N.C.R.. Cash Registrex, etc.) He clears the machine.
7. Prepares a statement of bills for those rooms whose bill crosses a specified amount.
8. He audits night receptionist's room report.
9. He checks the accuracy of accounts like over charging, under charging, cutting, discounts, allowances, etc. extended to uests.
10. He checks the City Ledger Account before transferring to Account Department for collection of bills.

The motive of night auditor is to rectify the error before guest checks out so that neither he is over charged nor under charged. This helps hotel'in improving its revenue and the image.

Night Auditor

A night auditor is a hotel employee who typically handles both the duties of the front desk agent and some of the duties of the accounting department. This is necessitated by the fact that most fiscal days close at or around midnight, and the normal workday of the employees in the accounting department does not extend to cover this time of day.

In larger hotels, night auditors may work alongside other nighttime employees, such as security officers, telephone attendants, room service attendants, and bellhops. In smaller hotels and motels, the night auditor may work alone, and may even only be "on-call", meaning that once he or she completes running the daily reports, the auditor retires to an area away from the desk while remaining available to attend to unexpected requests from guests.

Accounting Function

The night audit itself is an audit of the guest ledger. The guest ledger (or front office ledger or transient ledger) is the collection of all accounts receivable for currently registered guests. It can also be defined as the collection of all guest folios. A folio (billing receipt) is the account of an individual guest who is currently registered. The guest ledger is distinct from the city ledger, which is the collection of accounts receivable for non-registered guests (such as credit card companies). The purpose of the Night Auditor is, but not limited to: ensuring the accuracy of all financial information; gathering all needed paperwork to complete the audit. This will include pulling any or all checked-out guests registration cards, making sure all guests are checked-out in the system that should be checked-out.

One task of the night auditor is posting the day's room rate and room tax to each guest folio at the close of business (which usually occurs from midnight to 2 AM).

Second, the night auditor must ensure the accuracy of the charges to the guest folios. Ensuring that the sum of revenues due to accounts receivable from the various departments (i.e. Food & Beverage, Rooms, gift shop) found on the department control sheets equals the sum of the charges made to the guest folios.

The folios for guests who are scheduled to leave the next morning may be printed and delivered to the guests' rooms.

Most hotels currently use computerized property management systems (PMS) to help perform the night audit. This has significantly reduced the amount of time required to perform the audit, as well as the arithmetic skill required of the auditor. An audit for a 1,000-room hotel can be completed in an hour with a PMS, whereas it would have taken an eight-hour shift using previous generation of technology (the NCR 4200 mechanical system). Another duty of night auditors is to run daily management reports off the PMS. These include occupancy reports and calculations of average daily rate (ADR) and revenue per available room (Revpar).

Front Desk Function

In addition to the accounting function, night auditors may also be required to perform the typical front desk functions during the graveyard shift. These functions include check-in, check-out, reservations, responding to guest complaints, coordinating housekeeping requests, and handling any emergencies that may arise. Due to the nighttime shift, the clientele that the night auditor must deal with may be different than that of a typical front desk agent. At some properties, night auditors are known for frequent interactions with prostitutes, who tend to visit hotels at late hours for rendezvous with guests and the graveyard shift staff.

Night auditors usually work alongside a security officer to maintain a level of security during late-night hours for both night staff and guests.

Departmental Accounting

In hotel there are many departments, some of them are revenue producing departments and other, are non revenue producing departments: These non revenue producing departments are equally important as without them the other departments can not produced revenue.

But in departmental accounting we will study only those departments which are revenue producing departments. The department means a revenue producing department under the head departmental accounting.

The management is always keen to know the financial position of all revenue producing departments. They would like to know the gross profit, departmental profit and net profit of each department. It can be compared with budgeted profit and with previous years and other departments as well on knowing these details the management can decide whether department's functioning is efficient or not and if not then what corrective measures can be taken.

Methods to Know Department's Profit

The Management can follow Gross Profit Method, Department Profit Method and Net Profit Method to know the department's profitability.

Gross Profit Method

To know the gross profit cost of sale or food cost is deducted from the total department's sale. All other departmental and other expenses are ignored. The main advantage of this system is that it is very simple and can be taught without many efforts. The disadvantage of this system is that other expenses like salaries, wages, depreciation, lighting, air-conditioning, etc. are not analysed. This is the method most commonly used in hotel and catering establishments. It analysts opening stock + purchases- closing stock and sales i.e. items affecting the groos profit of each department. Sometimes a department makes a very good gross profit but when other expenses are debited it shows a loss.

Net Profit Method

All kinds of expenses which are directly or indirectly related to the department are debited to it e.g. The salary paid to kitchen staff is charged to food sale and salary paid to bar staff is debited to bar account and in case expenses are incurred for more than one department than the expenses are apportioned in the most suitable and fair manner to the departments so that almost the actual share of expenses are debited to each department. The expenses incurred on head office or corporate office is also suitable apportioned to debit the respective departments to know their net profit.

Some times the individual departments do very good business and make a reasonably good departmental profit but when other expenses, uncontrollable by departmental head are debited than department comes in red. Most of the public sector companies have this problem. Due to excessive head office, zonal office expenditure, even if individual department is in black it gets in red when uncontrollable departmental expenses are also debited. The biggest advantage of this method is that management can always know whether a particular department is making profit or not and if not then what is the reason whether departmental expenses are to be controlled or other expenses are to be checked. But this method is subject to many controversies. The departments are never satisfied the way the expenses are apportioned. Some times a department may close for renovation; it becomes difficult to ascertain that this department's over heads should be debited to whom. Some times a major marketing expenditure may have to be incurred for a new restaurant which has very low sale.

It is very difficult to say that which of this departmental accounting method is most suitable because each method has its own advantages and disadvantages. Management has to choose very carefully the most suitable method depending upon its needs.

Cost Allocation

The food service manager is able to make better decision if he is aware of the total cost of operation e.g. it seems obvious that food cost should be charged to the food sale and beverage cost to the beverage sale.

The *labour charges incurred by* the bar tender could be charged to the beverage service and salary paid to cook be charged to food sales. There are some common costs that can not be identified easily e.g. rent, light, water bill, laundry charges, telephone bill, etc. can not be assigned to any one individual department.

Cost allocation is nott discussed in any signification detail in the Uniform System of Accountancy. This cost can be allocated to the different departments depending upon various factors.

Advantages of Cost Allocation

The main advantage of cost allocation is that management knows the true financial position of each department and if so desired the management can take the corrective measure to make any particular department more efficient and control its overhead and other costs. In case the costs are not allocated to the respective departments and it is debited to the overall gross profit then management *may never come to know which department* is economically viable or not or which department is more viable and which is the least viable. The cost allocation also makes department more efficient and they also impose self control to show better financial results. The cost allocation helps individual Restaurant, Bar, Room, etc. to fix the selling price. The different outlets may operate on different food cost in order to cover their allocated over heads and other costs and still make a reasonable profit. With the knowledge of full costs of each department and may be for each banquet party the management can decide any revision in price or if the particular department is to be closed altogether. or if thee sales target are to be revised upwardly to cover the over heads and still make reasonable profit.

4

Hotel Accountancy Systems

Uniform accounts is used by several hotels/restaurants of the same accounting (costing and sales) principle and/or practices. Uniform accounting is thus not a separate technique or method. It simply denotes a situation in which number of hotels/restaurants may use the same accounting (costing and sales) principle in such a way as to produce costs and sales which are of maximum comparability because from such costs and sales, valuable conclusion can be drawn and one hotel can be compared to others. The extent of application of uniform accounting principles depends on the circumstances of each case.

Many schemes of uniform accounting system have been introduced in the last century and a few of them are still in use. The most successful uniform system of accounting was the one introduced by the Federation of Master Printers in 1911 and the most successful system in hotel industry was introduced in March 1926 by the Hotel Association of New York City and in September, 1926 the American Hotel and Motel Association of the North America adopted the same and recommended its members to adopt it. The success of Uniform Accounting System depends on the removal of the following difficulties.

1. Existence of Cooperation, mutual trust and a policy of give and take amongst the participating member hotels/ restaurants.
2. Free exchange of Ideas and Technology, knowledge amongst the member hotels/restaurants.

3. Free exchange of information regarding system of costing stocks, depreciation, etc.
4. Absence of rivalry and sense of jealousy amongst the member hotels/restaurants.
5. Use of common heads to record sales of hotel like Room Sale, Food Sale, Beverage Sale, Laundry Income, Telephone Income, Health Club and Swimming Pool Income, etc.
6. Use of common terminology and procedure regarding cost apportionment and cost control.

It may be noted the accounting system of hotels/restaurants may vary widely on the account of the following reasons

1. Size of Business : In a small hotel/restaurant/guest house, the owner with the help of family members may perform most of the function himself and he may use his personal kitchen for preparing food for the guests. Whereas, in large hotels the job is divided amongst departments and sections and cost allocation is required to be done differently.
2. Method of Production : Some small hotels may find it convenient to buy the food and beverage items from outside and sell it to the guests by adding their margin of profit. Whereas, large hotels find it more economical to cook themselves and serve it to guests.
3. Difference in Apportionment : There can be a large degree of difference in the accounting treatment of expenses, different bases of collection, absorption of overheads, method of depreciation, etc.

Where a Uniform Accounting System is introduced there must be some uniformity in the treatment of sales, expenses and general accounting procedures.

The following important matters require uniformity of treatment

1. Sales accounting policy and principle : The heads for different departments and outlets sales must be finalized so that each hotel and restaurant follows the same heads.

This will help in comparing the sales of one hotel with other.

2. General classification of accounts : There must be clear distinction about direct cost, indirect cost, food cost (variable cost), labour head, overheads, etc.
3. Allocation and apportionment of overheads : The hotels/ restaurants should be divided amongst suitable cost centres and the basis for the apportionment and allocation should be fixed so that all members follow the same principles. The overheads of the hotels/restaurants should also be absorbed uniformly.
4. The member hotels and restaurants under uniform accounting system should have the agreement on the following items

a) Method of depreciation and of pricing of material should be adopted.

b) If interest of capital should be debited and if so then on what basis.

c) If notional interest or rent should be charged on land and building owned by the hotel.

d) How wastages, complementary food served to guests and staff should be treated.

e) On what rate overtime, conveyance, etc. should be paid.

Advantages of Uniform Accounting System

The following are the advantages of Uniform Accounting System

1. Transfer : The staff can be transferred from one hotel to the other very easily as due to same accounting system it does not take long for the staff to adjust to the new hotel.
2. Comparison : Since hotels are following the same accounting system so they can be compared amongst each other. One can find out the causes for higher costs or lower sales and can take corrective measure.
3. Buying Shares : General public or financial institutions

can compare the hotels profitability and it helps them in deciding the price. They should pay to buy the equity, take over or to pay as a loan.

4. Lease or Rent : It is easy to decide on the rent or a lease for the hotels/restaurants. Both tenant and owner can study and compare the expenditure and income of various hotels/ restaurants and this will help to decide on the rental value or lease money for the hotel/restaurant on yearly or season basis.

As it has been discussed in the above that it is not easy to introduce Uniform Accounting System. In fact keeping in view, the heterogeneous industry like hotels, airlines, catering, restaurants, clubs, etc. and moreover, they are located at different places and of different sizes and providing different types of services, it becomes more difficult to have a Uniform Accounting System.

In India hotels to save income tax and other taxes do not at times show actual sale; on the contrary at times hotels show more sale then the actual to make the balance sheet look rosier. Due to high depreciation allowed hotel's in spite of showing more sale are able to save income tax and can convert black money to white money. Thus hotels do not follow the Uniform System of Accounting.

The following schedules are accepted by a group of restaurants to have uniformity in the accounting system. These schedules are as follow

- food sale
- beverage sale
- other income
- salary and wages
- employee's benefits
- direct operational expenses
- music and entertainment
- marketing expenses

- energy expenses
- administrative and general expenses
- repairs and maintenance
- rent and rates
- other expenses
- depreciation
- interest
- income tax.

Food Sale : Schedule D 1 for food sale is designed initially to show the number of meals served and amounts by meal period and secondly by dining area. Food sales include sales of tea, coffee, fresh juices, food, bakery products sold at restaurants, room service, banquets, etc.

Beverage Sale : This includes the sale of aerated drinks, canned juices, Beer, Wine, Cocktails, Hard drinks, etc. The beverage sale of bar, room service bar and beverage sale shown by other outlets is included and shown as Beverage Sale.

Other Income : Other income includes income from swimming pool, floweriest shop, health club, income from beauty parlour, etc. Net income means sale less cost of sale is shown as income under the head Other Income.

Income from rentals, interest and dividends earned should be shown as addition to income on the summary statement of income and should not be reported on this schedule.

Salary and Wages : Salary and wages paid to permanent staff, contractual staff and paid to porter for cartage should be included under the head salary and wages. The salary or remuneration paid to the owner is not included under the head salary and wages.

Employee's Benefits : Employee benefits include medical benefit or re imbursement, Contributory Provident Fund or Insurance Fund, Rent Allowance or Rent re imbursement, Leave Travel Concession, Children Education, Free or Subsidized Food, etc.

Direct Operational Expenses : Direct Operational Expenses include all those expenses which are incurred for providing services to the guests like linen, dry cleaning, table ware, kitchen utensils, fuel, stationery, power, etc. But this does not include food cost (variable cost) and direct labour cost.

Music and Entertainment : This includes salary and perks (conveyance, food, insurance, etc.) paid to musicians, rent paid for the equipments, money spend on the booking agent's fees or commission, money paid for procuring films, records, discs, etc. or royalty paid to companies for giving permission to play music in the restaurant or bar.

Marketing Expenses : Marketing expenses include selling, advertising (hoarding, print and electronic advertisement), fees and commissions, salary paid to marketing staff, donations, good will type expenditures, royalties, fees paid to franchisors, money spend on research and development, etc.

Energy Expenses : It includes electricity, heating expenses, water charges, ice and refrigeration supplies, waste removal, etc.

Administrative and General Expenses : The operational expenses like office expenses, stationery used in office, postage, telephone, travelling expenses (travelling not undertaken for the promotion of business), insurance, etc.

Repairs and Maintenance : This includes repair and maintenance of building, equipment like repair and white wash/ painting of building, repair of furniture and fixture, repair of kitchen equipments, etc. The money spend on repair should neither increase the production, nor improve the quality of product nor increase the life of asset substantially as this kind of expenditure is considered as capital expenditure and is not debited to repairs and maintenance account.

Rent and Rates : This includes rent and occupation costs, real estate taxes, property tax, building and machinery/equipments insurance, etc. Most of these expense are fixed in nature unless they are linked with sale e.g. the rent can be a certain percentage of sale and will vary depending upon the sale.

Other Expenses : The expenses which are not covered under any of the above mentioned heads are listed under the head other expenses.

Depreciation : In India depreciation is always shown separately as it is a statutory requirement to show profit before depreciation and interest. The Cash Earning Per Share includes the net profit plus depreciation.

Interest : It is very important for investor and general public to know the debt equity ratio of a company. The interest paid on the borrowed money is to be shown separately so the investor can know the financial health of the company.

IncomeTax : Th:? corporate are required to pay income tax on every penny they earn and are shown separately in the books.

Note

Cost of Goods Sold : The cost of raw material of food and beverages sold is termed as cost of goods sold. It is also called as Variable Cost and is deducted from the total sale to know the Gross Profit; some establishments term it as Net Sale as well.

To know the cost of sale the total of raw material consumed is totalled; the other way to find out the cost of goods sold is brought forward of food and beverage products add requisition from stores and deduct the balance in hand at the end of the day. The balance in hand becomes the brought forward on the following day. (To know in detail about cost of goods sold; please refer to 'D' part of this book)

Service Charges : Some hotels charge service charge in lieu of customary payment of tips. The service charge so charged is distributed to the staff and is not shown as sale.

There is no hard and fast rule that each group of company or association has to follow the' above mentioned schedule. The association/group may recommend another schedule depending upon their needs.

The income statement is the detail of revenues and expenses. The income statement provided to suppliers, debtors, creditors, bankers, etc. is different as compare to the income statement prepared for the management.

The income statement provided to management is much more in detail as compare to the income statement presented to suppliers, etc. Usually the income statement provided to management contains last three years revenues and expenses. The gross revenue information detail along with per share revenue like, EPS and CEPS (Earning Per Share, Cash Earning Per Share), profit, etc. is enclosed for the perusal of management and investors.

Income Statement

The summary of all accounts dealing with transactions relating to revenue and expenses is termed as profit and loss account. The account is termed as statement wherein information is accumulated relating to the item or group of items giving information regarding expenses and revenue.

Hotel Income Statements

Net Income = Revenues – expenses

- Revenue results from the sale of goods and services. It also includes interest income, dividend income, and other items reported on the schedule of rentals and other income.
- Expenses are the costs of goods and services used in the process of creating revenue.
- The net income does not necessarily cause a corresponding increase in the business's cash account. Therefore, net income is not cash flow.

Hotel Income Statement Formats

Income Statement Users

a) Internal Users;
   - Board of Directors
   - General Manager, President or CEO
   - Department and/or Division Heads
   - Supervisory Positions.

b) External Users;

- Government
- Credit-holders (I.e. Banks, Major Suppliers)
- Potential and Actual Investors.

Income Statement Formats:

- Internal long-form format
- Internal short-form format
- External formats.

1. Internal long-form format presents detailed information to the reader. It encompasses all departments' net revenue, cost of sales, payroll and related expenses, and other expenses and eventually the income or loss engendered from all operations.
2. Internal short-form format is a brief income statement format. It includes shortly the income (or losses) of revenue centres along with undistributed expenses, fixed charges, income tax, and eventually net income.
3. Common-size external format shows the relation-ship of each item in the income statement to net sales (as a percentage)
4. Comparative income statement presents and compares financial data for two or more periods (shown either in dollar amounts or percentages).

Why Income Statement shall be prepared first?

Income Statement shall be first prepared in order to know the Net Income, from which the Company must deduct Dividends Declared to reach Period's Retained Earning which will be accumulated in the Equity Section of the Balance Sheet!

Statement of Retained Earnings

- This very statement represents the lifetime profits (or losses) of a business that have not been declared as dividends to the shareholders. Moreover, this very statement is increased by the net income of the period and decreased by dividends declared for the period.

- Prepared in order to close the period's Net Income and to serve as the amount to be transferred to the Equity Section of the Balance Sheet!
- The Board of Directors' shall first meet and decide whether to distribute Dividends or not. If Dividends would be distributed.
- The Company is not obliged to pay immediately Dividends when they are declared. However, it is compulsory for the Company to pay them on the same Fiscal Year.

Reasons for Making Statement of Income

1. *Debt Servicing Cost :* Income statement helps company to know that whether they are in a position to recover the interest paid on borrowings from bank, market (both secured and unsecured loans) or not.
2. *Return on Investment :* It is very important to know whether the reasonable return is being paid to the investors, share holders both equity and preference or not. The company would also like to maintain different types of reserves like general reserve, capital reserve, special reserve, etc.
3. *Income :* To know Income, Company is making from routine, normal day-to-day operations.
4. *Success or Failure of Management :* Whether company is making reasonable returns from the capital deployed by them. If the returns are better then the competitors then the policies of the management are considered as successful.
5. *Popular :* Whether the goods or/and services offered by the company are popular in the market or not. If the sale is improving or is better then the competitors then it is considered that the services/goods offered are popular.
6. *Price Sensitivity :* The impact on the sale by increasing or reducing the price is known from income statement and this helps management in deciding whether to increase or reduce the rate and by what percentage.

7. *Profit Centred or Volume Centred* : The price sensitivity helps management in deciding that the policy of the management should be price centred or volume centred. The high volume of sale will give a lower percentage of profit as compare to low volume of sale. The volume of sale will increase if the price of the product is reduced. At times by reducing the price the volume of sale is increased considerably and the management makes more profit even if the percentage profit on sale is lower.

Detailed Study of Income Statement Revenue Earning Departments

1. Lettable rooms
2. Food and Beverage
3. Swimming Pool and Health Club 4. Floweriest and Beauty Parlour
5. Telephone and Secretariat Services 6. Other Operated Departments 7. Rental and Lease Income.

Undistributed Department Expenses

1. Operation Expenses
2. Administrative and General Expenses
3. Salary and Wages
4. Sales and Marketing Expenses 5. Fuel and Energy Cost

Fixed Expenses

1. Rent and Lease
2. Interest
3. Depreciation and amortigation
4. Insurance
5. License Fee.

Balance Sheet-Uniform System of Accounts

The Balance Sheet also known as 'The Statement of Financial Position', contains the assets, liabilities and net worth of a hotel/

company at the end of accounting period or at any given point of time (generally end of the years, half years, quarterly or monthly). If a balance sheet is prepared one day after the previous balance sheet than it will give a slightly different picture about assets, liabilities and net worth.

The financial information is useful for different reasons. The following are the important reasons for preparing the Balance Sheet.

1. One can know the current assets like Cash in Hand, Cash at Bank, Stock, Bills Receivable, etc. and compare them with the current liabilities like Sundry Creditors, Bills Payable, Short Term Loans, Outstanding Payments, etc. One can see whether hotel is able to pay the current liabilities or not, or if there is liquid crunch,
2. Most of the assets of the hotels are of fixed in nature. The balance sheet explains about all these assets.
3. Long Term Loans of both secured and unsecured nature is listed on the liabilities side of balance sheet. Higher the debt-equity ratio, more interest burden the hotel has to bear and it affects adversely on the profit of the hotel.
4. Different types of reserves show that whether earning is retained by the hotel for future growth. The capital reserve and special reserve are the indications for the hotels financial stability and capacity to pay for secured and unsecured loans.
5. One can see whether all authorised capital of hotel has been issued and subscribed or not and whether equity capital or. preference capital is authorised, issued and subscribed and if both types of capital are issued then what is the ratio and what is the dividend to be paid for preference shares and if any other conditions are attached to the preference shares.

The balance sheet (Account Form) has been discussed in detail in earlier part of this book. The students may note that in North America the left side of balance sheet is called 'Assets' and right side as 'Liabilities'. Where as, in India the left side is called

'Liabilities' and right side 'Assets'. Balance Sheet (Report form) is discussed in this chapter.

Limitations of Balance Sheet

Though balance sheet is one of the most important instruments of financial accountancy but still it has certain limitation. *The following are the limitations:*

1. It is based on transactions recorded in accordance with GAAP (Generally Accepted Accounting Principles). The land and building is recorded in the balance sheet at cost price, the price of building is depreciated every year and the depreciated value of building like other assets is recorded. The present value of the land might be much more then that of book value of land (cost price of land) but this appreciated value of land can not be shown in the balance sheet so it does not give the real value of assets.
2. The Rupee is depreciating regularly. The imported equipment purchased three years ago might have more value in terms of Indian Rupees but this increased value can not be shown in balance sheet.

These two reasons can be corrected by putting a foot note just below the balance sheet. The three major Indian Hotel Chains viz East India Hotel (E.I.H.-Oberoi), Indian Hotels (Taj Hotels), ITC Hotels (Welcome Group of Hotels) have much more actual value then shown in the balance sheet because the properties purchased many years ago have much more value then the book value shown in the balance sheets. The goodwill is shown in the books only when a price is paid for acquiring the goodwill. The three major Indian hotel chains have acquired goodwill with their own efforts and performance so they are not showing any goodwill in the book. Any buyer who is interested in buying these equities (shares) wants to know the real value of assets and goodwill before taking a final decision.

Contents of the Balance Sheet

Assets:

The Assets of a hotel can be divided into the following parts:

1. Current Assets
2. Fixed Assets
3. Deferred Revenue Expenses
4. Investments
5. Non Tangible and Other Assets.

Current Asset : Currents assets are those assets which can be converted to cash at a short time of say six months to one year. Current assets are listed in the order of liquidity. These are:

a) *Cash :* Cash means total cash in hand at Front Office, Restaurant, Bar, Health Club, Swimming Pool, Cashier, Petty Cashier including imprest money sanctioned to all cashiers.

b) *Bank:* Cash balance with all the banks along with the cheques, drafts deposited but not collected as yet and cash being deposited in the bank. From this total, the total amount of cheques issued but not presented as yet for payment is to be deducted.

c) *Sundry Debtors :*They are all those persons to whom credit has been extended and the account department is sending them bills for payment. These sundry debtors are usually those people who have stayed in the hotel and signed at the time of check out or paid through credit cards. In case the hotel is of the view that any part of these debtors might not pay due to any reason then from these debtors expected bad debts are deducted and the net amount is written in the amount column against sundry debtors.

d) *Closing Stock :* Closing stock means the stock of all kitchens and restaurants material whether kept in kitchens/ restaurants or store is recorded in the closing stock.

e) *Bills Receivable :* In case'bills or promissory notes are issued to any person then these are also recorded in the current assets.

f) *Advance Salaries and Other Expenses :* Sometimes hotel pays advance salary to employees for some reason. The rent, insurance premium, commission, etc. might have been paid in advance without being due then this is shown as current assets and is adjusted as and when it becomes due.

Fixed Assets : Fixed assets are those tangible assets, which are beneficial to hotel for more then one year and it must have a substantial value. Some hotels may not consider any assets of less then Rs. 5,000 as assets even if it has value for more then one year. e.g. buckets bought for hotel may have more then one year life but are still not considered as assets because of their low monetary value.

Each fixed asset, may be with the exception of land, depreciates due to wear and tear as the time passes. So the depreciation is charged to each fixed asset and the depreciated value of the asset is shown in the balance sheet under the head fixed assets. The following are the fixed assets and are listed in the order of liquidity.

a) *Furniture and Fixture :* The hotels have large assets in the form of furniture and fixture. Each bed room, bath room, restaurant, bar, stores, lobby, etc. have a lot of furniture and fixture fittings.

b) *Machinery:* It includes Kitchen, Bar, Restaurant, House keeping equipments. It also includes cutlery, laundry equipment, centralized heating and air-conditioning, etc.

c) *Land & Building :* If the building is purchased then it must also include the brokerage charges, registration fee and the value of the land and building should be shown separately in the books. But if the building is constructed then the entire material, labour, consultancy, supervisory, architect cost should be debited to building account. If the old building is purchased and is renovated before starting the hotel then renovation cost should also be added to building account.

Deferred Revenue Expenses : Sometimes hotel makes major revenue nature expenditure and it gives a utility to the hotel for more then one year and due to limited profit it is not written off in the financial year when it is incurred. There is no hard and fast rule that what types of expenditure should be treated as deferred revenue expenditure. The following are the most common deferred revenue expenditures

a) *Major Renovation : A* hotel is usually renovated after a few years to stay in the business and to make it more comfortable to guests. A large amount of money is spending on the renovation of the hotel and hotel does not require any major expenditure on renovation for next couple of years. The accountant show a part of the renovation expenditure in current financial year's profit & loss account and the balance is shown as an asset under the head deferred revenue expenditure and is written off in the next three to four years.

b) *Advertisement :* Whenever a new hotel or a new restaurant is opened a large amount is spending on its publicity so that awareness can be created in the market about the new property. Usually this expenditure is of large amount and this advertisement gives benefit to hotel for many years to come and hence the expenditure is shown as deferred revenue expenditure.

c) *Pre-Opening Expenses :* Sometimes hotels make large pre-opening expenses in the form of advertisement, soft opening, etc. and these expenses are also shown as deferred revenue expenses in balance sheet.

Note : 1. Pre-opening expenses can be capitalised.

Major Renovation Expenses can be Capitalised, if Hotel Increases the Tariff after Renovation

***Investment:** In* case hotel has surplus cash and does not have any expansion plan for the time being, decides to invest it in the form of fixed deposits, debentures or buy shares of other public limited company to earn some revenue for the hotel. These investments are bought in the name of the company and are shown in the balance sheet. These different investments are discussed in detail in later part of this book.

Non Tangible & Other Assets : Non tangible are those assets which can neither be seen nor felt as they have no shape but have value like Goodwill, Patent, etc. Other assets are security paid for water connection, Gas connection, Power connection or Bar license or Hotel license fee. When goodwill or patent is bought from another person then only it is shown because one may pay some money towards goodwill, patent fee, etc. But if the goodwill, patent is earned with own efforts of business then it is not shown in the books. It may have a value in the eye of a buyer but it is not shown in the balance sheet.

Liabilities

The amount which is due to others on the date of writing balance sheet is listed under the head liabilities. The total of assets side and liabilities side is always the same. In other words:

Assets = Liabilities + Capital or

Capital = Assets-Liabilities

The liabilities can be divided into four parts

Current Liabilities : Current liabilities are-those liabilities which are to be paid within a year. These are:

a) *Sundry Creditors* :The hotel buys stock and equipment from suppliers and usually does not make cash payment. These suppliers are paid within one month to six months depending upon the terms and conditions and hotel's policy.

b) *Bills Payable: In case a bill was accepted from someone then the value of the* bill is settled in 30 days and is shown as a current liability.

c) *Advance Received :* At the time of room reservation or part booking an advance is received for confirming the booking and is adjusted against the bill as and when it is raised. Till the amount is adjusted, this advance is shown as a liability against advance received.

d) *Unpaid Expenses :* In case some expenses like rent, interest, commission, *salary, etc. is due but not paid as yet is shown as a liability in the balance* sheet. This liability may be paid almost immediately.

e) *Short Term Loans :* Some times hotel takes short term loans to meet the demands of recurring expenses. Usually these loans attract high rate of interest and have to be paid within a year.

f) *Dividend Payable :* The dividend declared but not paid due to unavoidable reasons is listed as a liability in the balance sheet.

Long Term Liabilities : These are those liabilities which need not be paid within one year or in other words it has to be paid after two to five years. These loans are taken for capital expenditure. The hotel must keep this loan amount as low as possible to keep the interest burden. within limits. The long term liabilities are:

a) *Long Term Loans* :.These loans are taken from banks, financial institutions or from public and are to be repaid after two to five years or may be more.

b) *Debentures :* Sometimes hotel issue debentures to collect money from the market for a long term. The debentures are to be paid back in two to four installments in three to ten years and more.

Reserves & Surplus : The hotel does not distribute all its profit to share holders but some profit of it is retained as surplus. The hotel may also earn some money on selling assets or sell shares at premium or may create special kind of reserve for some specific purposes. Whatever may be the reason, the reserve is a cash with the hotel and can be used for the development and expansion. Broadly reserves are of three types:

a) *General Reserve* :The undistributed profit is transferred to reserve account. This reserve is maintained so that hotel can pay dividend on subsequent years even if there is not sufficient profit or this reserve is used for the expansion of business.

b) *Capital Reserve* :This reserve cannot be used for paying dividend to share holders and is created on selling the assets at over and above the book value or by selling shares at premium. This can be used for acquiring assets or for expansion of business.

c) *Special Reserve* :This reserve is created to pdy back certain liabilities which will be due for payment after one to three years. These reserves are created from the profit of the hotel operations.

Capital : The hotels have two types of Share Capital and these are Equity Share Capital and Preference Share Capital.

a) *Equity Share Capital & Preference Share Capital :* Equity shares are the shares which are issued to the share holders. These share holders get profit only if there is surplus earning from the business. The preference share holders get a minimum of certain fixed dividend even' if there is no earning.

The other Types of Capital are;

i) *Authorised Share Capital :* It is that amount of capital which a hotel can issue to the public. The hotel may or may not issue all the capital it is authorised to issue. In case the hotel wants to increase the authorised capital then it has to obtain the approval of share holders and intimate the decision of share holders to SEBI.

ii) *Issued Share Capital :* It is that amount of capital which is issued to the public through prospectus. The Board of Director may or may not issue all the authorised capital to the public for subscription.

iii) *Subscribed Capital :* All the issued capital may or may not be subscribed by the public. But if public does not subscribe 90% of the issued capital within the stipulated time then Board of Directors are required to return the money to subscribers and no share can be allotted.

Responsibility Accounting

A hospitality business with several departments, each with the responsibility for controlling its own costs and with its department head accountable for the departmental profit achieved, is practicing what is known as responsibility accounting. Responsibility accounting is based on the principle that department heads or managers should be held accountable for their performance and the performance of the employees in their department. There are two objectives for establishing responsibility centres:

1. Allow top-level management to delegate responsibility and authority to department heads so they can achieve departmental operating goals compatible with the overall establishment's goals.
2. Provide top-level management with information (generally of an accounting nature) to measure the performance of each department in achieving its operating goals.

Within a single organization practicing responsibility accounting, departments can be identified as cost centres, revenue centres, profit centres, or investment centres. A cost centre is one that generates no direct revenue (such as the maintenance department). In such a situation, the department manager is held responsible only for the costs incurred.

Some establishments also have revenue centres. These departments receive sales revenue, but have little or no direct costs associated with their operation.

For example, a major resort hotel might lease out a large part of its floor space to retail stores. The rent income provides revenue for the department, all of which is profit.

A profit centre is one that has costs but also generates revenue that is directly related to that department. The rooms department is an example where the manager is responsible for generating revenue from guest room sales. The manager of a profit centre should have some control over the sales revenue it can generate. Thus, profit centres are responsible for both maximizing revenue and minimizing expenses, which, in turn, maximizes departmental profit. Each profit centre manager or department head can then be measured on how well profit was maximized while continuing to maintain customer service levels established by top-level management.

In both cost and profit centres, a key question is, what costs should be assigned to each centre? Generally, only those costs that are directly controllable by that centre's department head or manager are assigned. The final type of responsibility centre occurs in a large or chain organization with units located in several different towns or cities. Each unit in the organization is given full authority over how it operates and is held responsible for the results of its decisions. In a large organization such as this, each unit is said to be *decentralized* and units are sometimes referred to as investment centres. Investment centres are measured by the rate of return their general managers achieve on the investment in that centre.

Transfer Pricing

In some chain organizations, products are transferred from one unit to another.

For example, in a multiunit food organization, raw food ingredients might be purchased and processed in a central commissary before distribution to the individual units. A question arises about the cost to be transferred to each unit for the partially or fully processed products. Many different pricing methods are available. It is important that an appropriate pricing method be decided so each unit can be properly measured on its performance.

For example, the transfer price could be the commissary's cost plus a fixed percentage markup to cover its operating costs. Another method might be to base the transfer price on the market price of the products.

The market price would be what the receiving unit would have paid if it had purchased the products from an external supplier. In some cases, the market price might be reduced by a fixed percentage to reflect the commissary's lower marketing and distribution costs. Obviously, each user unit would prefer to have the transfer price as low as possible so its costs are lower, and the commissary would prefer to have the transfer price as high as possible to enhance its performance.

Distribution of Indirect Expenses

One controversial issue concerning the income statement is whether the indirect expenses should be distributed to the departments. The problem arises in selecting a rational basis on which to allocate these costs to the operating departments. Some direct expenses might also have to be prorated between two operating departments on some logical basis. For example, an employee in the food department serving food to customers might also be serving them alcoholic beverages.

The food department will receive the credit for the food revenue, the beverage department for the beverage revenue. However, it would be unfair for either of these two departments to have to bear the full cost of that employee's wages.

That cost should be split between the two departments, possibly prorating it on the basis of the revenue dollars. Such interdepartmental cost transfers are easily made; they are necessary to have a reasonably correct profit or loss for each operating department for which the appropriate department head is accountable.

One of the arguments in favor of allocating indirect expenses to departments is that, although departmental managers are not responsible for controlling those costs, they should be aware of what portion of them is related to their department since this could have an impact on departmental decision making, such as establishing selling prices at a level that covers all costs and not just direct costs.

When this type of full-cost accounting is implemented in a responsibility accounting system, it allows a manager to know the total minimum revenue that must be generated to cover all costs, even though the control of some of those costs is not their responsibility.

Some undistributed indirect expenses can be allocated easily and logically.

For example, marketing could be distributed on a revenue ratio basis. However, if a particular advertising campaign had been made specifically for one department, and it was thought that little, if any, benefit would accrue to other departments, then the full cost of that campaign could reasonably be charged to that one department as a direct cost.

Internal Control

The control is a continuous process. It is a part of routine in all types of organisations, whether small or big. The word 'control' itself is disliked by one and all, nobody likes to be controlled by others no matter how small or big employee he may be.

Definition

"The whole system of control, financial and otherwise, established by the management in order to carry on the business of the enterprises in an orderly and efficient manner, ensure adherence to management policies, safe-guard the assets and secure as far as possible the completeness and accuracy of the records".

Scope/Objectives of the Internal Control

1. To check frauds and thefts.
2. To safeguard the assets of the business from thefts and misuse (cutlery and small equipments).
3. To improve the efficiency.
4. To follow the policies of the management.
5. To improve the quality.
6. To complete the records up to moment.

Essential Features/Types of Internal Control

1. Experienced, Qualified and Trustworthy Personnel
2. Division of Duty
3. Leadership
4. Organisational Structure
5. Sound Practice
6. Authorise Personnel
7. Records
8. Manual Procedure
9. Control
10. Budget
11. Reports

12. Independent Checks:

1. *Experienced, Qualified and Trustworthy Personnel* : The personnel should be well qualified, experienced and trustworthy and this helps in providing better services than competitors. This also ensures in having a better internal control on pilferages.

2. *Division of Duty* : The duties are segregated to improve the efficiency, quality and for controlling the pilferage.

3. *Leadership* : Board of Directors, General Manager and other managers and supervisors must lead the person by communicating the policies of the hotel to one and all and encourage the personnel to have the best out put and control.

4. *Organisational Structure* : The Chain of hotels or hotel as the case may be must have a clear organisational structure and the personnel must know from whom to take orders and to whom to report.

5. *Sound Practice* : These are policy measures generally set up and implemented by the board of directors and other senior executives in order to create an environment which facilitates internal control.

6. *Authorise Personnel* : The management must authorize clearly the personnel for taking certain decision. For example: a person should be authorised to extend discount, cancel a bill, extend complementary food/ room, etc.

7. *Records* : The records must be maintained to ensure internal control The records like guest registration cards, bills, K.O.T.'s, control sheets, etc. are not only maintained, checked, verified, but are also stored for future references.

8. *Manual Procedures* : Each job should be reduced to writing. Log books must be maintained in each department. The Manual Procedures should list the details of each position including how and when to perform each task.

9. *Control* : Control includes security services and measures for protecting assets, *(253)* stores, guest's valuables, etc. The security services, as far as possible, must be hired from professionals.
10. *Budget* : The Budgets like short term, long term, specific budgets, etc. must be made for sale, cost, production, etc. The budgets must be achievable but not achievable so easily. The goals of the hotel must be clearly mentioned and the goals must be made not only for sale, cost, etc. but must also be made for controlling pilferages.
11. *Reports* : For each job reports must be made and circulated among the executives of the hotel for information and control.
12. *Independent Checks* : The personnel responsible for performing the jobs should not be asked for the internal checks but internal checks must be performed by different personnel either from the permanent personnel employed in the hotel or some times may be hired from out side.

The internal control is all the more important in hospitality industry. In normal business houses; the sale is carried out for a limited period of eight to ten hours a day and almost all the sale is made from a sale counter managed by the owner himself or by his confident.

But in Hotel Industry, the cash as well as credit sale is made from various outlets and that too 24 hours a day and 365 days a year. At hotels we sell different kind of food and beverage products both produced at various kitchens of the hotel end procured from outside. We also sell various types of services like health club, swimming pool, beauty parlour, secretariat services, telephone services, and travel services and so on.

These sales are made to both in house guests and outsiders. Keeping in view the above facts it becomes very important that we have an affective control over these outlets sales. It is not always possible to have a management eye watching cashiers and other staff members engaged in selling various services, presenting check (bill), settling bills and returning back the balance and receipts.

To ensure that staff does not get tempted to pilferage the cash sales, certain control procedures are developed for the restaurant/bar/other departments sales.

The instruments used for the Food and Beverage Service Control are as follows;

1. Kitchen Order Ticket (K.O.T.)
2. Restaurant Check.
3. Restaurant Sales Summary Sheet.
4. Kitchen Summary Sheet.
5. Guest Weekly Bill.
6. Visitor's Tabular Ledger (V.T.L.).

Kitchen Order Ticket (K.O.T.)

The four copies of K.O.T. are made. The order is taken by the captain on K.O.T. The original copy of the K.O.T. is given to Aboyer (Barker) to place the order. After the food has been picked up by the pick-up waiter, this copy of the K.O.T. is kept in the locked K.O.T. Box, which is taken by the control department at the end of the day or shift for control purposes.

The first carbon copy is given to cashier so that he can make the check. The second carbon copy is given to pick up waiter so that he can pick up the food from the kitchen. The last copy is kept at the side board (dummy waiter) for the reference of captain or stewards and this helps in service.

Restaurant Check

Restaurant Check is either prepared by cashier or waiter but is usually priced and totalled by cashier. To pick-up the food, the check is shown by pick up waiter and the check items are ticked by barker before giving the food. On demand, all the four copies of the check are presented to the guest, either he pays'in cash or he signs and puts his name and room number or he settled his bill through credit card or debit card. If he pays in cash than the original copy of the check is returned to him with the stamp of paid and cashiers signature as a receipt, but in case he signs as a resident or as a credit card holder than original copy is send to front office and the first carbon copy is given to the guest for his reference. The second carbon copy is send to accounts department and the third, carbon copy is for control department.

In case a restaurant check is lost by the waiter than he is liable to pay Rs. 1,000 as a fine along with the price of the check (The check's price can be ascertained with the help of K.O.T.) In case a check is lost by the cashier then he is liable to pay the fine instead of waiter. When a check is issued to the waiter, he is required to sign in the Restaurant's sales summary sheet and when he returns the check to cashier he takes the stub duly signed by the cashier as a proof that he has returned the check to the cashier.

Restaurant Sales Summary Sheet

On this summary sheet cashier maintains the complete record of restaurant sales. When he issues a check to pick up waiter, he gets his signature and when he (waiter) returns the check to the cashier than the lower perforated portion of the check (stub), along with cashier's signature and stamp, is returned to the waiter and this is his proof that he has returned the check to the cashier.

In case this check is lost than the responsibility is fixed on cashier or waiter and who-so-ever is held responsible, is required to pay the price of the check and a fine of Rs. 1,000. The restaurant sales summary sheet is prepared in duplicate and a copy each is send to the accounts department and control department.

In case guest settles his bill in cash than the amount received is shown in the cash column and discount allowed is shown in the discount column. In case the guest settles his bill by signing (either as a hotel resident or as a credit card/debit card holder) than the total amount is shown in the ledger column and in the remarks column the Room Number, Name of the Guest, Credit Card Number/Debit Card Number and other details are entered. Cashier signs in the Signature column.

Kitchen Summary Sheet

The Chef prepares a Kitchen Summary Sheet with the help of K.O.T's. This is also known as **Kitchen Cost Sheet.** This summary sheet is prepared in duplicate and a copy each is send to the Accounts Department and the Control Department.

Guest Weekly Bill

For each resident of the hotel a guest weekly bill/guest bill is prepared. All debit and credit vouchers along with room tariff are posted in this bill and as soon as guest desires to check out this bill is presented to him for settlement.

For control purposes a copy each of this is send to control department and accounts department. But the original copy, in case of cash payment, is given to the guest as his receipt. In case guest signs the bill than original bill copy is send to the company for collection by accounts department and the bill is transferred to Ledger accounts and transferred to Account Department for collection.

Visitor's Tabular Ledger

For all the hotel residents of a day a Visitor's Tabular Ledger is prepared. It is also known as **Day Book.** For every day a new ledger is prepared.

On this ledger the room rent and all the vouchers for all the guests are recorded. The Visitor's Tabular Ledger gives the total sale of the residents of the hotel (but the cash paid by residents in restaurants is not recorded here). A copy each of this ledger is send to the control department and accounts department.

Visitor's Tabular Ledger

In case the hotel has the computerized accounting system than the restaurant sales summary sheet, guest weekly bill, kitchen summary sheet and visitor's'tabular ledger are automatically made and the control department can have their printouts on their computers. In some hotels a separate K.O.T. is not prepared; the restaurant check is prepared by machine/computer. The monitor of kitchen shows the order and a K.O.T. in leaf form is not given to barker. For ordering the food there is no need to show the check because order is only placed through computer if check is prepared.

Cash Control

As it has been already discussed in 'Restaurant Sales Conter I' that cash sales are made at various outlets throughout the day and night. A hotel ay make a couple of lakhs of Rupees cash sale in a day.

A cashier may be tempted to run away with the cash. To have an affective control of cash the hotel's management usually do not appoint a cashier unless and until they are very sure about his credentials and they take minimum of two references. Usually cashiers are rotated very regularly from one outlet to the other and head cashier keeps a watch on them.

All the cash collected by cashier is deposited to the front office cashier along with sales summary sheet. The imprest amount given to cashier is checked quite regularly by head cashier/ accountant/control department.

The cashiers are not allowed to keep imprest money with them but is also deposited/kept at hotel or handed over to the cashier of next shift. All the check books are numbered and in case of any cuttings the checks must be counter signed by the manager. The front office cashier is required to prepare a cash book. All the cash received must be banked. Except front office cashier, who may be required to make petty cash payments on behalf of resident guests against visitor paid out, no other cashier is authorized to pay from the cash sales.

Cash Receipts and Payments/Disbursements

It is very important to control the cash receipts and cash payments/disbursements. No doubt in hotel industry it is becoming more and more common to settle the bills through vouchers/credit facilities extended to regular customers and through credit or debit cards but still a good number of guests settle their bills in cash. Moreover the cash is received throughout the day and night and at various cash counters spread in different parts of the hotel.

Cash Receipts

Cash receipts must be controlled from the point of sale till it is banked. The following steps are followed for its control

1. Checks must be prepared for each cash receipt and a proper receipt must be handed over to the guest.
2. The Checks must be numbered and tearing, cutting or canceling of check must be signed by an authorised manager.
3. All Checks must be entered in the Sales Summary Sheet.
4. The total cash received must be deposited in the bank immediately after the shift is over or instantly when there is cash more then the recommended cash in the cash chest. The cash should be deposited by each cashier him self or it should be deposited by the Front Office Cashier. But the Front Office Cashier must issue a receipt to each cashier on receiving the cash from them. The cash so received by Front Office Cashier must be shown in the Cash Book.
5. Each cashier should be given a float/imprest for paying balance to guests or for encashing foreign currencies (Only Front Office Cashier is authorised to accept foreign currency from guests). The float so handed over to the cashiers must be checked both at the end of the shift and during the shift (surprise check). The cashier should not be allowed to keep the float with them after the shift is over and the float should be deposited with the Front Office Cashier or should be handed over to the next shift's cashier.
6. The allowances/discounts/complementary should be only extended and signed by the authorised personnel.
7. The un used checks must be kept under lock and key and the serial numbered checks are issued to the cashiers against their signatures.

Cash Payments/Disbursements

This includes control over purchases, expenses and salary payments. As far as possible the cash payments should not be encouraged. All payments must be made by cheques. As far as possible the hotel must avoid making cash payments, however, petty payments may be made, in cash by petty cashier. The cheque must be kept under lock and key and cheque payments must be made after verifying the bills, supply order, purchase order, invoice, store keeper's report, etc.

Salary should be disbursed by making a direct payments to the employee's account opened in the hotel's bank. Before making the salary payments the attendance from the department and time office must be taken into account. For larger amount cheques, if possible, two authorized persons must sign the cheque. The cash book must be kept ready up to moment and must be signed daily by an authroised person. The bank reconciliation statement must be prepared on weekly or fortnightly basis.

Types of Internal Control

The following are the main types of internal control

1. Organisation
2. Division of Duties
3. Physical Control
4. Supervision
5. Financial Accuracy.

Organisation : The management must make the organization chart of all the departments. The authorities, responsibilities, reporting to, must be clearly identified; each job must be clearly described and specified. In case of delegation of power, it should be in writing with the approval of superiors. It must be clear to superiors that the authority/power can be delegated to subordinates but the responsibility can not be delegated.

The superiors are always responsible for the deed and misdeeds of subordinates. In larger hotels a lot of power is delegated to juniors because one person can not perform all the duties. In smaller hotels the owner himself supervises almost every thing. The organization chart of a hotel may differ from hotel to hotel, depending upon the size of the motel, policy of the hotel, mechanical devices available, etc.

Division of Duties : The duties among different employees must be divided to have an affective control; but in smaller hotels, the broad division of duties may not be possible. For example, in a large hotel the bill clerk and cashier can be separate person; this will have a control of one person over other and less chances of cash pilferage.

Physical Control : In hotels the security is assigned to an outside agency so that security guards and hotel staff do not become friendly. All the departments, when not in operation must be locked and key, after sealing, must be kept with the security officer. The employees must use only staff gate for coming and leaving the hotel.

This gate must be manned by a security officer round the clock. Each staff member must be checked physically to ensure that they are not taking away hotel's property, may be by mistake, like match boxes, hand towels, knife, etc. The stores must be locked after normal working hours and no unauthorized person should be allowed to enter. The cash book, keys, cheque books, etc. must be kept in safe custody of responsible person.

Supervision :The supervisors must authorize/approve all the transactions of the hotel. All cutting/over writing must be counter signed. The power of the supervisors must be specified in writing to avoid confusion.

Financial Accuracy: The totals, calculations, pricing of each bill must be checked for its accuracy. The over charging and under charging are very bad for the hotel. The bank account must be reconciled on weekly basis. The checks and K.O.T.'S must be numbered. At the end of every month ledgers must be balanced and trial balance prepared.

With the modern accounting techniques developed, the arithmetic accuracy *is* ensured by machines.

To ensure the affective internal control, the staff must be regularly trained. It is rightly said that training is a continuous process, every employee must be trained for a minimum of 100 hours in a year. The new employees must be imparted training before putting them on the actual job. The old staff knowledge must be updated and in case of shifting to new systems/methods the staff must be trained and motivated. The supervisors and management must ensure that the systems developed by the hotel must be followed by every one and this will always ensure the perfect internal control.

In hotels, a separate internal control department is made under the direct supervision of Chief Controller who reports to General Manager. The primary job of internal control is to help management discharge their responsibilities. The nature and extent of control will depend upon business to business. It will also depend upon nature, size and volume of transactions and the policy of the management.

In spite of the best efforts of management, supervisors and control department, it is never possible to eliminate pilferage altogether. Management always bears in mind the cost of control and the benefits derived from them. Like any other departments operation, internal control department's functions must be regularly reviewed to ensure its *usefulness.*

The following situations must be checked;

1. The staff refuses transfer or promotion.
2. The staff neither wants weekly off nor leaves.
3. The staff has bad evils like gambling, loitering and spending heavily. 4.
   Close relation with suppliers.
5. Close friendship with cashiers, store keeper, kitchen/ restaurant staff.
6. Staff is very close to superiors or control department employees.

Major Types of Frauds

The internal control system is not only designed to prevent and detect fraud, but also to prevent and detect error which is usually more common than fraud. Though it is very difficult to list down all kinds of fraud, in fact every moment some where in the world, a new type of fraud takes place.

Some of the common frauds are:

1. Failure to make K.O.T.
2. Failure to make Check
3. Failure to record sales in Sales Summary Sheet
4. Under recording of sale
5. Picking up of food without proper check
6. Collecting payment from guest without check
7. Charging incorrect room rent
8. Selling room without registration
9. Payment of bill twice
10. Receiving a bill without goods
11. Receiving bills twice for one supply
12. Receiving goods and bill without any purchase order
13. Allowance or discount allowed without proper authorization
14. Ghost pay rolls
15. Full payment made for substandard goods received 16. Stealing hotels inventory and assets.

Usually the owner himself supervises the small number of employees and he has a thorough knowledge of the inventory and assets kept in the hotel. Moreover the quantity of inventories and assets are very limited.

The following steps are recommended for small hotels control.

1. Either use cash book and bill book or use machine operated cash register.
2. The double entry system of book-keeping should be followed.
3. The cash books bank column must be compared with pass book and bank reconciliation statement prepared on monthly basis.
4. The budget must be prepared and all actual figures must be compared with budgeted figures.

5. As far as possible he must sign cheques himself after verifying the purchase order, invoice, etc.
6. All cuttings must be counter signed by himself or by some one authorized by him.
7. Cash payments must be avoided as far as possible.

Limitations of Internal Control

1. The persons authorized to control may themselves involve in fraudulent.
2. Two employees (for example: waiter and cook) may join hands in fraudulent.
3. Due to shortage of staff or over load of work.
4. Human error due to bad judgment
5. Carelessness.

5

Budgeting Hospitality Industry

Policy Statement

The capital improvements program includes all capital projects, regardless of size, financed with state and University funds, and all departmentally funded projects exceeding $100,000 (see the Special Situations section for information on projects less than $100,000). The capital improvements program is an ongoing process that includes:

- Assessing capital needs, opportunities and resources
- Ensuring that potential projects conform with academic priorities & investment strategies
- Establishing priorities for project funding.

Provosts, Chancellors and Vice-Presidents submit their capital improvement needs for review by the Capital Improvements Advisory Committee which recommends systemwide priorities to the Senior Officers of the University. The President submits the capital budget to the Regents.

Exclusions

Purchases of free-standing instructional and research equipment, even those large enough to be categorized as a "capital expense", should be funded through the operating budget, and should not be submitted to the capital budgeting process. None of the funding sources available for allocation through the capital budget are available for free-standing equipment purchases.

Special Situations

Self-funded projects of less than $100,000 do not require individual approval by the Regents, and are, therefore, excluded from the capital budget process. These projects are handled as follows:

1. Projects are initiated by submitting a Form 1395 request to Capital Planning and Project Management with the dean's sign-off that the proposed project:
   * Conforms with academic priorities of the University
   * Has adequate funding identified
2. Projects are briefly reviewed to ensure that the proposed project:
   * Is within a facility worth investment
   * Will not significantly increase the cost of maintaining and operating the facility
   * Addresses code compliance issues
   * Causes no negative impact on adjacent space/facilities
   * Conforms with campus master planning principles
3. Projects that meet the preceding criteria will be scheduled for implementation immediately. Projects that do not appear to satisfy all of these criteria will be referred to the CIAC for review and recommendation, and to the Senior Officers for concurrence.
4. If during the planning and design stage the cost of a project increases beyond the $100,000 threshold, the project will be considered in the next capital budgeting cycle, or if the need is urgent, it may be handled as an amendment to the capital budget, requiring the review and recommendation of the CIAC, the concurrence of the Senior Officers, and the approval of the Regents.

Purchases of free-standing instructional and research equipment, even those large enough to be categorized as a "capital expense", should be funded through the operating budget, and should not be submitted to the capital budgeting process. None of the funding sources available for allocation through the capital budget are available for free-standing equipment purchases.

However, if the equipment purchases require adjustments to building systems (examples: expanded electrical capacity, HVAC modification) or remodelling of space, those facility improvements should be submitted to the capital budgeting process in accordance with the definitions regarding project size and funding source contained in Section C. A department purchasing equipment which requires building adjustments must either invest departmental funds to achieve those modifications, or must request central funds through the capital budgeting process.

If the purchase of equipment represents a high programmatic priority, the priorities for distributing capital resources may be influenced.

Reason for Policy

To assist the President in preparing the capital budget and capital improvements program. To facilitate informed investment decisions and promote effective management of existing capital assets.

Submitting a Project for the Capital Budget

Procedure

Types of Projects

All projects meeting the following definitions must be submitted to the capital budgeting process:

- Projects requesting central or state funding, regardless of size. Central and state funding sources include fire and life safety, ADA improved access, hazardous materials abatement, repair and replacement, program accommodation remodelling, internal loans, central reserves, University bonds and state bonds.
- Self-funded projects which exceed $100,000. Self-funding sources include departmental funds (O&M, ISO, ICR, gifts and grants) and fees collected by self-supported auxiliary services.

Academic units should submit only projects related to their programmatic needs. Projects that relate exclusively to fire and life safety, improved access, hazardous material abatement, or repair and replacement, should be referred to the units, listed below, that are responsible for addressing those needs.

Type of Improvement-Responsible Unit

Fire and Life Safety-University Building Official.

ADA access-Facilities Management TC Campus FM or Plant Services on other campuses. Hazardous material-Environmental Health and Safety / TC abatement Campus and air quality FM or Plant Services on other campuses.

Repair and replacement-Facilities Management on TC Campus FM or Plant Services on other campuses.

Submitting A Project

Submit capital projects to the capital budgeting process in the following manner:

- Departments identify a capital need, complete a project identification form, and submit it to the College or Resource Responsibility Center (RRC). Attach a copy of the project identification form.
- Colleges/RRCs review the requested capital improvement, assign a priority ranking to the request, and submit it to the Provost/Chancellor/Vice President.
- Provosts/Chancellors/Vice Presidents review the requested capital improvement, assign a preliminary priority ranking to the request, submit it to the Office of Budget and Finance, and present it to the Capital Improvements Advisory Committee (CIAC) budget hearings.

Project Identification Form

A project identification form must be submitted for all projects proposed for the period, including projects which were previously submitted and incorporated into the Capital Improvements Program. Each annual capital budget and capital improvements program is treated as a new undertaking, and confirmation of each project and its priority ranking is required if it is to remain in the capital improvements program.

Project identification forms for projects included in the current capital improvements program are being returned to the Provosts, Chancellors, and Vice Presidents with instructions. Persons proposing those projects may obtain the forms from their Provost, Chancellor, or Vice President in order to improve the project information. If there are no changes, simply resubmit the sheets.

Project Identification Forms must be submitted by Oct. 31, 1996 CAPITAL BUDGET

To be considered for inclusion in the Capital Budget, the following conditions must be satisfied:

- Proposed construction projects must have a comprehensive cost estimate prepared by or under the direction of Capital Planning and Project Management. Proposed land or facility acquisitions must have an appraisal approved by the Real Estate Office.
- Proposed projects must have funding available, or have funding contingent upon a pending grant application or private gifts from an active fund raising campaign.

Unless both of these conditions are satisfied, the project will not be included in the Capital Budget, but will instead be placed in a future fiscal year of the capital improvements program.

Prior to Regents' approval of the capital budget, the Office of Budget and Finance will verify the availability of funding for projects which are dependent upon State and University funds. Departments and auxiliaries will be asked to verify the availability of funding for projects to be financed with departmental funds or with fees collected by self-supported auxiliaries by providing a CUFS account number, or by identifying a Foundation account, a grant application, or a fund raising effort.

Verification of funding must be received annually by April 1.

Projects must be identified during the annual budgeting process if they are to be considered for inclusion in the Capital Budget.

Projects which are not identified at this time will be deferred to next year's budgeting cycle. Only in extraordinary circumstances will projects be considered as amendments to the approved capital budget during the course of the year. Budget amendments require special review and recommendation by the CIAC, concurrence by the Senior Officers, and approval by the Board of Regents. Implementation of a project cannot proceed until it has been included in the capital budget.

Equipment Purchases

Purchases of free-standing instructional and research equipment, even those large enough to be categorized as a "capital expense", should be funded through the operating budget, and should not be submitted to the capital budgeting process. None of the funding sources available for allocation through the capital budget are available for free-standing equipment purchases.

However, if the equipment purchases being considered will require adjustments to building systems (examples: expanded electrical capacity, HVAC modification) or remodelling of space, those facility improvements should be submitted to the capital budgeting process in accordance with the definitions regarding project size and funding source described at the beginning of this procedure. A department purchasing equipment which requires building adjustments must either invest departmental funds to achieve those modifications, or must request central funds through the capital budgeting process. If the purchase of equipment represents a high programmatic priority, the priorities for distributing capital resources may be influenced.

Discussion Issues and Derivations

Working Capital, Net Working Capital and Non-Cash Working Capital

Working capital is sometimes used to refer only to current assets, while net working capital is defined to be the difference between current assets and current liabilities. Non-cash working capital looks at the difference between non-cash current assets and current liabilities.

In investment analysis, increases in working capital are viewed as cash outflows, because cash tied up in working capital cannot be used elsewhere in the business and does not earn returns. It is the "does not earn returns" component of this definition that would lead us to look at non-cash working capital. Firms with significant cash balances today, especially in the US, earn market returns on their cash (by investing in at least T.Bills). Thus, the cash is productive and changes in the cash should not affect our cash flows.

To the degree that cash cannot be invested to earn market returns, and is needed for day-to-day operations, it is appropriate to look at changes in net working capital, with cash included.

Operating versus Capital Expenditures

Accountants draw a distinction between expenditures that yield benefits only in the immediate period or periods (such as labour and material for a manufacturing firm) and those that yield benefits over multiple periods (such as land, buildings and long-lived plant). The former are called operating expenses and are subtracted from revenues in computing the accounting income, while the latter are capital expenditures and are not subtracted from revenues in the period that they are made. Instead, the expenditure is spread over multiple periods and deducted as an expense in each period-these expenses are called depreciation (if the asset is a tangible asset like a building) or amortization (if the asset is an intangible asset like a patent or a trade mark).

While the capital expenditures made at the beginning of a project are often the largest and most prominent, many projects require capital expenditures during their lifetime. These capital expenditures will reduce the cash available in each of these periods.

Depreciation, Amortization and Other Non-cash Charges

The distinction that accountants draw between operating and capital expenses leads to a number of accounting expenses, such as depreciation and amortization, which are not cash expenses. These non-cash expenses, while depressing accounting income, do not reduce cash flows. In fact, they can have a significant positive impact on cash flows, if they affect the tax liability of the firm. Some non-cash charges reduce the taxable income and the taxes paid by a business. The most important of such charges is depreciation, which, while reducing taxable and net income, does not cause a cash outflow. Consequently, depreciation is added back to net income to arrive at the cash flows on a project.

For projects that generate large depreciation charges, a significant portion of the cash flows can be attributed to the tax benefits of depreciation, which can be written as follows

Tax Benefit of Depreciation = Depreciation * Marginal Tax Rate

While depreciation is similar to other tax deductible expenses in terms of the tax benefit it generates, its impact is more positive because it does not generate a concurrent cash outflow.

Amortization is also a non-cash charge, but the tax effects of amortization can vary depending upon the nature of the amortization. Some amortization, such as the amortization of the price paid for a patent or a trade mark, are tax deductible and reduce both accounting income and taxes. Thus, they provide tax benefits similar to depreciation. Other amortization, such as the amortization of the premium paid on an acquisition (called goodwill), reduces accounting income but not taxable income. This amortization does not provide a tax benefit.

Capital Expenditures and Depreciation

In project analysis, it is important that assumptions about capital expenditures, depreciation and working capital be consistent. For instance,

- If the project is assumed to have a very long life or an infinite life, the firm will have to make much larger capital maintenance expenditure. As a simple rule of thumb, when projects have infinite life, the capital maintenance expenditures should approach depreciation. This will, if nothing else, ensure that the book value of the investment does not decline. More importantly, it is necessary to preserve the earning power of the assets

- For projects with shorter lives, it is possible that capital expenditures occur up front, and that depreciation in subsequent years is much greater than capital expenditure. The book value of the investment will decline over time to the salvage value.

ROC, Cost of Capital, NPV and EVA

Economic value added is a value enhancement concept that has caught the attention of both firms interested in increasing their value and portfolio managers, looking for good investments. EVA is a measure of dollar surplus value created by a firm or project and is measured by doing the following:

Economic Value Added (EVA) = (Return on Capital-Cost of Capital) (Capital Invested)

where the return on capital is measured using "adjusted" operating income, where the adjustments eliminate items that are unrelated to existing investments, and the capital investment is based upon the book value of capital, but is designed to measure the capital invested in existing assets. Firms which have positive EVA are firms which are creating surplus value, and firms with negative EVA are destroying value.

In the context of investment analysis, the present value of the EVA created by a project should be equal to the net present value of the project.

ROE, Cost of Equity and Equity EVA

While EVA is usually calculated using total capital, it can be easily modified to be an equity measure:

Equity EVA = (Return on Equity-Cost of Equity) (Equity Invested in Project or Firm)

Again, a firm which earns a positive equity EVA is creating value for its stockholders while a firm with a negative equity EVA is destroying value for its stockholders.

Equity EVA may be the better way of thinking about value created for firms where capital is tough to measure (such as banks and insurance companies).

Equity Analysis versus Firm Analysis

An investment project can be analyzed in terms of all of the capital invested in the project (firm) or just from the perspective of the equity investors in the firm. If done consistently, cash flows to the firm discounted at the cost of capital or cash flows to equity discounted at the cost of equity, the two approaches should yield similar results if the following conditions hold:

a. The project is financed using the same mix of debt and equity as is used in the computation of the cost of capital.

b. The debt is assumed to have an interest rate equal to the pre-tax cost of debt

Currency Effects on Investment Analysis

One of the debates that analysts often engage in when doing investment analysis is whether the analysis should be done in one currency or another. Intuitively, an analysis of whether a project is a good or bad one should not depend upon what currency the analysis is done in. The important fact to keep in mind is that cash flows and the discount rate have to be estimated consistently. To convert the analysis from one currency to another would have required the following steps:

Step 1: Estimate the expected exchange rate for each period of the analysis.

While forward rates might be available for some currencies for a few periods, there are very few cases where forward rates will be available for the entire project life. To estimate the expected exchange rate, draw on the purchasing power parity theorem that argues that changes in exchange rates between two countries will reflect differences in inflation in those countries.

Step 2: Convert the expected cashflows from one currency to the other in future periods, using these exchange rates.

Step 3: Discount the expected cashflows at a discount rate, based upon the same currency.

Real versus Nominal Investment Analysis

Investment analyses can be done in terms of real or nominal

cash flows. The discount rates have to be defined consistently-real for real cash flows and nominal for nominal cash flows. If done consistently, each analysis should yield the same net present value.

The choice between nominal and real cash flows therefore boils down to one of convenience. When inflation rates are low, it is better to do the analysis in nominal terms since taxes are based upon nominal income. When inflation rates are high and volatile, it is easier to do the analysis in real terms.

Given a choice, I would rather do the analysis in nominal terms, since taxes and financial statements are usually based upon nominal results.

Net Present Value, IRR or Modified IRR

For firms with no capital rationing constraints, net present value is clearly the choice that will maximize firm value the most. For firms with significant capital rationing constraints that will continue into the future, the IRR is likely to be the best solution. For firms with significant capital rationing constraints that will ease over time, the modified IRR is the best solution.

Corporate Strategy and Project Quality

In the process of analyzing new investments in the preceding chapters, we have contended that good projects have a positive net present value and earn an internal rate of return greater than the hurdle rate. While these criteria are certainly valid from a measurement standpoint, they do not address the deeper questions about good projects including the economic conditions that make for a "good" project and why it is that some firms have a more ready supply of "good" projects than others.

Implicit in the definition of a good project--one that earns a return that is greater than that earned on investments of equivalent risk--is the existence of super-normal returns to the business considering the project. In a competitive market for real investments, the existence of these excess returns should act as a magnet, attracting competitors to take on similar investments. In the process, the excess returns should dissipate over time; how quickly they dissipate will depend on the ease with which competition can enter the market and provide close substitutes and on the magnitude of any differential advantages that the business with the good projects might possess. Take an extreme scenario, whereby the business with the good projects has no differential advantage in cost or product quality over its competitors, and new competitors can enter the market easily and at low cost to provide substitutes. In this case the super-normal returns on these projects should disappear very quickly.

An integral basis for the existence of a "good" project is the creation and maintenance of barriers to new or existing competitors taking on equivalent or similar projects. These barriers can take different forms, including

a. *Economies of Scale*: Some projects might earn high returns only if they are done on a "large" scale, thus restricting competition from smaller companies. In such cases, large companies in this line of business may be able to continue to earn super-normal returns on their projects because smaller competitors will not be able to replicate them.

b. *Cost Advantages*: A business might work at establishing a cost advantage over its competitors, either by being more efficient or by taking advantage of arrangements that its competitors cannot use. For example, in the late 1980s, Southwest Airlines was able to establish a cost advantage over its larger competitors, such as American and United Airlines by using non-union employees, the company exploited this cost advantage to earn much higher returns.

c. *Capital Requirements*: Entry into some businesses might require such large investments that it discourages competitors from entering, even though projects in those businesses may earn above-market returns. For example, assume that Boeing is faced with a large number of high-return projects in the aerospace business. While this scenario would normally attract competitors, the huge initial investment needed to enter this business would enable Boeing to continue to earn these high returns.

d. *Product Differentiation*: Some businesses continue to earn excess returns by differentiating their products from those of their competitors, leading to either higher profit margins or higher sales. This differentiation can be created in a number of ways-through effective advertising and promotion (Coca Cola), technical expertise (Sony), better service (Nordstrom) and responsiveness to customer needs.

e. *Access to Distribution Channels*: Those firms that have much better access to the distribution channels for their products than their competitors are better able to earn excess returns. In some cases, the restricted access to outsiders is due to tradition or loyalty to existing competitors. In other cases, the firm may actually own the distribution channel, and competitors may not be able to develop their own distribution channels because the costs are prohibitive.

f. *Legal and Government Barriers*: In some cases, a firm may be able to exploit investment opportunities without worrying about competition because of restrictions on competitors from product patents the firm may own to government restrictions on competitive entry. These arise, for instance, when companies are allowed to patent products or services, and gain the exclusive right to provide them over the patent life.

Management and Project Quality

In the preceding section we examined some of the factors that determine the attractiveness of the projects a firm will face. While some factors, such as government restrictions on entry, may largely be out of the control of incumbent management, there are other factors that can clearly be influenced by management may largely be out of the control of incumbent management, there are other factors that can clearly be influenced by management. Considering each of the factors discussed above, for instance, we would argue that a good management team can increase both the number of and the returns on available projects by

- taking projects that exploit any economies of scale that the firm may possess; in addition, management can look for ways it can create economies of scale in the firm's existing operations.

- establishing and nurturing cost advantages over its competitors; some cost advantages may arise from labour negotiations, while others may result from long-term strategic decisions made by the firm. For instance, by owning and developing SABRE, the airline reservation system, American Airlines has been able to gain a cost advantage over its competitors.
- taking actions that increase the initial cost for new entrants into the business; one of the primary reasons Microsoft's was able to dominate the computer software market in the early 1990s was its ability to increase the investment needed to develop and market software programs.
- increasing brand name recognition and value through advertising and by delivering superior products to customers; a good example is the success that Snapple experienced in the early 1990s in promoting and selling its iced tea beverages.
- nurturing markets in which the company's differential advantage is greatest, in terms of either cost of delivery or brand name value. In some cases, this will involve expanding into foreign markets, as both Levi Strauss and McDonalds did in the 1980s in order to exploit their higher brand name recognition in those markets. In other cases, this may require concentrating on segments of an existing market as The Gap did, when it opened its Banana Republic division, which sells upscale outdoor clothing.
- improving the firm's reputation for customer service and product delivery; this will enable the firm to increase both profits and returns. One of the primary factors behind Chrysler's financial recovery in the 1980s was the company's ability to establish a reputation for producing quality cars and minivans.
- developing distribution channels that are unique and cannot be easily accessed by competitors. Avon, for instance, employed large sales force to go door-to-door to reach consumers who could not be reached by other distribution channels.

- getting patents on products or technologies that keep out the competition and earn high returns; doing so may require large investments in research and development over time. It can be argued that Intel's success in the market for semiconductors can be traced to the strength of its research and development efforts and the patents it consequently obtained on advanced chips, such as the Pentium.

While the quality of management is typically related to the quality of projects a firm possesses, a good management team does not guarantee the existence of good projects.

In fact, there is a rather large element of chance involved in the process; even the best laid plans of the management team to create project opportunities may come to naught if circumstances conspire against them-a recession may upend a retailer, or an oil price shock may cause an airline to lose money.

Working Capital Management

Defining Working Capital

The term working capital refers to the amount of capital which is readily available to an organisation.

That is, working capital is the difference between resources in cash or readily convertible into cash (Current Assets) and organisational commitments for which cash will soon be required (Current Liabilities).

Current Assets are resources which are in cash or will soon be converted into cash in "the ordinary course of business".

Current Liabilities are commitments which will soon require cash settlement in "the ordinary course of business".

Thus:

WORKING CAPITAL = CURRENT ASSETS-CURRENT LIABILITIES

In a department's Statement of Financial Position, these components of working capital are reported under the following headings:

Current Assets

- Liquid Assets (cash and bank deposits)
- Inventory
- Debtors and Receivables

Current Liabilities

- Bank Overdraft
- Creditors and Payables
- Other Short Term Liabilities

The Importance of Good Working Capital Management

Working capital constitutes part of the Crown's investment in a department. Associated with this is an opportunity cost to the Crown. (Money invested in one area may "cost" opportunities for investment in other areas.) If a department is operating with more working capital than is necessary, this over-investment represents an unnecessary cost to the Crown. From a department's point of view, excess working capital means operating inefficiencies. In addition, unnecessary working capital increases the amount of the capital charge which departments are required to meet from 1 July 1991.

Approaches to Working Capital Management

The objective of working capital management is to maintain the optimum balance of each of the working capital components. This includes making sure that funds are held as cash in bank deposits for as long as and in the largest amounts possible, thereby maximising the interest earned. However, such cash may more appropriately be "invested" in other assets or in reducing other liabilities.

Working capital management takes place on two levels:

- Ratio analysis can be used to monitor overall trends in working capital and to identify areas requiring closer management.
- The individual components of working capital can be effectively managed by using various techniques and strategies.

When considering these techniques and strategies, departments need to recognise that each department has a unique mix of working capital components. The emphasis that needs to be placed on each component varies according to department. For example, some departments have significant inventory levels; others have little if any inventory.

Furthermore, working capital management is not an end in itself. It is an integral part of the department's overall management. The needs of efficient working capital management must be considered in relation to other aspects of the department's financial and non-financial performance.

Financial Ratio Analysis

Financial ratio analysis calculates and compares various ratios of amounts and balances taken from the financial statements.

The main purposes of working capital ratio analysis are:

- to indicate working capital management performance; and
- to assist in identifying areas requiring closer management.

Three key points need to be taken into account when analyzing financial ratios:

- The results are based on highly summarised information. Consequently, situations which require control might not be apparent, or situations which do not warrant significant effort might be unnecessarily highlighted;
- Different departments face very different situations. Comparisons between them, or with global "ideal" ratio values, can be misleading;
- Ratio analysis is somewhat one-sided; favourable results mean little, whereas unfavourable results are usually significant.

However, financial ratio analysis is valuable because it raises questions and indicates directions for more detailed investigation.

The following ratios are of interest to those managing working capital:

- working capital ratio;
- liquid interval measure;
- stock turnover;
- debtors ratio;
- creditors ratio.

Working Capital Ratio

Current Assets divided by Current Liabilities

The working capital ratio (or current ratio) attempts to measure the level of liquidity, that is, the level of safety provided by the excess of current assets over current liabilities.

The "quick ratio" a derivative, excludes inventories from the current assets, considering only those assets most swiftly realisable. There are also other possible refinements.

There is no particular benchmark value or range that can be recommended as suitable for all government departments. However, if a department tracks its own working capital ratio over a period of time, the trends-the way in which the liquidity is changing-will become apparent.

Liquid Interval Measure

Liquid Assets divided by Average Operating Expenses

This is another measure of liquidity. It looks at the number of days that liquid assets (for example, inventory) could service daily operating expenses (including salaries).

Stock Turnover

Cost of Sales divided by Average Stock Level

This ratio applies only to finished goods. It indicates the speed with which inventory is sold-or, to look at it from the other angle, how long inventory items remain on the shelves. It can be used for the inventory balance as a whole, for classes of inventory, or for individual inventory items.

The figure produced by the stock turnover ratio is not important in itself, but the trend over time is a good indicator of the validity of changes in inventory policies.

In general, a higher turnover ratio indicates that a lower level of investment is required to serve the department.

Most departments do not hold significant inventories of finished goods, so this ratio will have only limited relevance.

Debtor Ratio

There is a close relationship between debtors and credit sales to third parties (that is, sales other than to the Crown). If sales increase, debtors will increase, and conversely, if sales decrease debtors will decrease.

The best way to explain this relationship is to express it as the number of days that credit sales are carried on the books:

Credit Sales per Period x Days per Period

Average Debtors: Where trading terms are 30 days net cash, and customers buy from day-to-day during the 30 day period and pay 30 days after a statement is rendered, a collection period of 45 days (the average between 30 and 60 days) would be satisfactory.

If the average collection period extends beyond 60 days, debtors are holding cash that should have flowed into the department. This means that the department is unable to satisfy pressing liabilities or to invest that cash.

The debtor ratio does not solve the collection problem, but it acts as an indicator that an adverse trend is developing. Remedial action can then be instigated.

Creditor Ratio

This ratio is much the same as the debtor ratio. It expresses the relationship between credit purchases and the liability to creditors. It can be stated as the number of days that credit purchases are carried on the books.

Credit Purchases per Period × Days per Period

Average Creditors: Note that non-credit purchases (such as

salaries) and non-cash expenses (such as depreciation) need to be excluded from "credit purchases" and any provisions need to be excluded from "creditors".

There is no need to pay creditors before payment is due. The department's objective should be to make effective use of this source of free credit, while maintaining a good relationship with creditors.

As with debtors, if a department has been granted credit terms of 30 days net cash, credit purchases should not be carried on the books for more than an average of 45 days. If payment is withheld for 60 days or more it is likely that creditors will become impatient and impose stricter and less convenient trading terms-for example, "cash on delivery".

The Public Finance Act 1989 (section 49) places a legal constraint on the amount of credit allowed to a department. It restricts to a maximum of 90 days the purchase of goods and services through the use of a credit card or suppliers' credit.

Specific Strategies

Inventories

Inventories are lists of stocks-raw materials, work in progress or finished goods-waiting to be consumed in production or to be sold.

The total balance of inventory is the sum of the value of each individual stock line. Stock records are needed:

- to provide an account of activity within each stock line;
- as evidence to support the balances used in financial reports.

A department also needs a system of internal controls to efficiently manage stocks and to ensure that stock records provide reliable information.

Departmental financial reports show only the total inventory balance. Analysts from outside the department can examine this balance by using ratio analysis or other techniques. However, this gives only a limited assessment of inventory management and is not adequate for internal management. Good financial management necessitates the careful analysis of individual inventory lines.

Inventory management is an important aspect of working capital management because inventories themselves do not earn any revenue. Holding either too little or too much inventory incurs costs.

Costs of carrying too much inventory are:

- opportunity cost of foregone interest;
- warehousing costs;
- damage and pilferage;
- obsolescence;
- insurance.

Costs of carrying too little inventory are:

- stockout costs:
    * lost sales;
    * delayed service.
- ordering costs:
    * freight;
    * order administration;
    * loss of quantity discounts.

Carrying costs can be minimised by making frequent small orders but this increases ordering costs and the risk of stock-outs. Risk of stock-outs can be reduced by carrying "safety stocks" (at a cost) and re-ordering ahead of time. The best ordering strategy requires balancing the various cost factors to ensure the department incurs minimum inventory costs. The optimum inventory position is known as the Economic Reorder Quantity (ERQ).

There are a number of mathematical models (of varying complexity) for calculating ERQ. (Any standard accounting text will provide examples of these).

Analytical review of inventories can help to identify areas where inventory management can be improved. Slow moving items, continual stockouts, obsolescence, stock reconciliation problems and excess spoilage are signals that stock lines need closer analysis and control.

However, it is important to keep an overall perspective. It is not cost-effective to closely manage a large number of low value inventory lines, nor is it necessary. A usual feature of inventories is that a small number of high value lines account for a large proportion of inventory value.

The "80/20" rule (PARETO) predicts that 80% of the total value of inventory is represented by only 20% of the number of inventory items. Those high value lines need reasonably close management. The remaining 80% of inventory lines can be managed using "broad-brush" strategies.

The overall management philosophy of an organisation can affect the way in which inventory is managed.

For example, "Just In Time" (JIT) production management organises production so that finished goods are not produced until the customer needs them (minimising finished goods carrying costs), and raw materials are not accepted from suppliers until they are needed. (Large organisations have the power to insist that suppliers hold stocks of raw materials and thereby pass the carrying cost back to the supplier).

Thus, JIT inventory strategies reduce bottlenecks and stock holding costs.

In summary:

- There is a trade-off to be made between carrying costs, ordering costs, and stockout costs. This is represented in the Economic Reorder Quantity (ERQ) model.
- Inventories should be managed on a line-by-line basis using the 80/20 rule.
- Analytical review can help to focus attention on critical areas.
- Inventory management is part of the overall management strategy.

Debtors

Debtors (Accounts Receivable) are customers who have not yet made payment for goods or services which the department has provided. The objective of debtor management is to minimise the time-lapse between completion of sales and receipt of payment. The costs of having debtors are:

- opportunity costs (cash is not available for other purposes);
- bad debts.

Debtor management includes both pre-sale and debt collection strategies.

Pre-sale strategies include:

- offering cash discounts for early payment and/or imposing penalties for late payment;
- agreeing payment terms in advance;
- requiring cash before delivery;
- setting credit limits;
- setting criteria for obtaining credit;
- billing as early as possible;
- requiring deposits and/or progress payments.

Post-sale strategies include:

- Placing the responsibility for collecting the debt upon the center that made the sale;
- Identifying long overdue balances and doubtful debts by regular analytical reviews;
- Having an established procedure for late collections, such as
    - a reminder;
    - a letter;
    - cancellation of further credit;
    - telephone calls;
    - use of a collection agency;
    - legal action.

Creditors

Creditors (Accounts Payable) are suppliers whose invoices for goods or services have been processed but who have not yet been paid. Organisations often regard the amount owing to creditors as a source of free credit. However, creditor administration systems are expensive and time-consuming to run. The overriding concern in this area should be to minimise costs with simple procedures.

While it is unnecessary to pay accounts before they fall due, it is usually not worthwhile to delay all payments until the latest possible date., Regular weekly or fortnightly payment of all due accounts is the simplest technique for creditor management.

Electronic payments (direct credits) are cheaper than cheque payments, considering that transaction fees and overheads more than balance the advantage of delayed presentation. Some suppliers are reluctant to receive payments by this method, but in view of the substantial cost advantage (and the advantages to the suppliers themselves) departments may wish to encourage suppliers to accept this option.

However, electronic payments are likely to be used in conjunction with, rather than as a replacement for, cheque payments.

Cash and Bank

Good cash management can have a major impact on overall working capital management.

The key elements of cash management are:

- cash forecasting;
- balance management;
- administration;
- internal control.

Cash Forecasting: Good cash management requires regular forecasts. In order for these to be materially accurate, they must be based on information provided by those managers responsible for the amounts and timing of expenditure. Capital expenditure and operating expenditure must be taken into account. It is also necessary to collect information about impending cash transactions from other financial systems, such as creditors and payroll.

Balance Management: Those responsible for balance management must make decisions about how much cash should at any time be on call in the Departmental Bank Account and how much should be on term deposit at the various terms available.

There are various types of mathematical model that can be used. One type is analogous to the ERQ inventory model. Linear programming models have been developed for cash management, subject to certain constraints. There are also more sophisticated techniques.

Administration: Cash receipts should be processed and banked as quickly as possible because:

- They cannot earn interest or reduce overdraft until they are banked;
- Information about the existence and amounts of cash receipts is usually not available until they are processed.

Where possible, cash floats (mainly petty cash and advances) should be avoided. If, on review, the only reason that can be put forward for their existence is that "we've always had them", they should be discontinued. There may be situations where they are useful, however. For example, it may be desirable for peripheral parts of departments to meet urgent local needs from cash floats rather than local bank accounts.

Internal Control: Cash and cash management is part of a department's overall internal control system. The main internal cash control is invariably the bank reconciliation. This provides assurance that the cash balances recorded in the accounting systems are consistent with the actual bank balances. It requires regular clearing of reconciling items.

Other Components

Working capital, defined as the difference between current assets and current liabilities, may also include the following factors:

- prepayments to creditors;

- current portions of long-term liabilities;
- revenue received before it has been earned;
- provisions.

However, decisions on working capital management usually exclude these factors, so they have not been included in this booklet.

Summary

Good management of working capital is part of good financial management. Effective use of working capital will contribute to the operational efficiency of a department; optimum use will help to generate maximum returns.

Ratio analysis can be used to identify working capital areas which require closer management. Various techniques and strategies are available for managing specific working capital items.

Debtors, creditors, cash and in some cases inventories are the areas most likely to be relevant to departments.

6

Financial Management in Hospitality Industry

Introduction

When you stayed in that luxury hotel during your last vacation, did you check what your neighbour paid for her room? If she were a business visitor, she could have paid well above $300 for the same room that you paid $180. It is also possible that she paid $120 provided she planned well in advance and managed to get that "better" deal which was elusive to you. So why do hotels charge different customers different rates for the same type of room? Such differences are the result of an increasingly common strategy to maximize revenue (and profits) in the Hotel industry–a practice referred to as Revenue or Yield Management.

Revenue Management (RM) is a scientific technique that combines Operations Research, Statistics and Customer Relationship Management (CRM) and categorizes customers into price bands, based on various services. Statistical analysis of past data helps in forecasting demand and establishing the appropriate price bands. Applied correctly, Revenue Management helps hotels expand market size and increase revenues. Some industry practitioners also refer to RM as the art of selling the right room to the right customer at the right time and for the right price.

To understand the need for an RM system, let us take the following two examples. At the peak of the SARS epidemic in Canada, a resort experienced a 25% drop in number of visitors. Amazingly, this resort managed to limit decline in revenue to a bare 3%. During economic depression, a travel management company reduced its marketing budget by half, but still managed a revenue increase of 6%. How were these successes possible? The answer to both of these questions lies with the implementation of Revenue Management strategy.

Why Revenue Management?

- *Segmented Market:* Hotels typically segment their market (customer base) into a set of categories based on the price each category is willing to pay. Typical categories include the business traveler and the vacation traveler. Because demand patterns for each of these categories may vary significantly, hotels find it difficult to satisfy all of the demand simultaneously. A good example is the comparison between the time-conscious business executive and the price-sensitive vacation customer. The former is willing to pay a higher price in exchange for flexibility of being able to book a room at the last minute while the latter is willing to give up some flexibility for the sake of a more inexpensive room. RM tries to maximize revenues by managing the trade-off between a low occupancy and higher room rate scenario (business customers) versus a high occupancy and lower room rate (vacation customers). Such a strategy allows hotels to fill rooms that would otherwise have been empty.
- *Fixed Capacity*: A hotel's capacity is relatively fixed-it is nearly impossible to add or remove rooms based on fluctuations in demand. If at all hotel capacity were flexible, there would be no need to manage capacity.
- *Perishable Inventory*: In the hotel industry, hotel rooms are the inventory. A hotel room that remains unoccupied for a night loses all its value for that night. This inventory cannot be stored and is lost forever. Because RM tries to manage demand instead of supply, it proves to be good business sense for the hotel.
- *Low Marginal Cost*: The fixed cost of adding a room in a hotel is heavily capital intensive. However, once the hotel

manages to cover its initial fixed costs, the cost of serving an additional customer is low enough that the hotel can sell the room at a lower margin if it wishes. Such a strategy will obviously need to be balanced by one that also seeks to sell the room(s) at higher margins. Thus, the high fixed cost/low marginal cost nature of the business makes price differentiation a necessity-something that is made possible by application of RM.

- *Advanced Sales*: More often than not, requests for bookings start early. Therefore, hotels have enough leeway to adjust room prices based on the variation between realized bookings and expected demand. If all hotel rooms are sold at the same time, the hotel does not have the flexibility to adjust prices upward if demand picks up later. The trade-off occurs when a manager is faced with the option of accepting an early reservation from a customer who wants a low price, or waiting to see if a higher paying customer will eventually show up...
- *Demand Fluctuations*: Demand for hotel rooms is characterized by crests and troughs, which the hotel factors in during the room pricing process. In peak season, the hotel can increase its revenues by raising room prices, while during lean seasons it can increase its utilization rate by lowering prices. Past data will offer the manager a way to forecast when these periods of high and low demand may occur. Unfortunately, it is very difficult to predict the actual demand with a high degree of certainty.

Therefore, the most critical challenge facing the hotel industry is predicting potential capacity, and developing a pricing strategy that will encourage maximum capacity and revenue.

Revenue Management is the most effective technique to solve this challenge, similar to aggregate and hierarchical production planning techniques often employ~d in the manufacturing industry.

Revenue Management is based on complex optimization methodologies developed from advanced statistical and analytical models.

In order to arrive at a solution, managers need to evaluate several millions of decisions, which requires a significant investment of skills, hardware and time. Many RM practitioners prefer to breakdown the actual business scenario into four sub-problems, and then identify an individual solution to some or all of these sub-problems.

This would significantly reduce the number of potential non-optimal decisions thereby providing fewer choices, leading to quicker results.

These four sub-problems are:

(a) Forecasting and Pricing,

(b) Market segment identification,

(c) Inventory allocation, and

(d) Overbooking.

How does it all Work?

Demand Forecasting

The next step in an RM process is forecasting demand and pricing of the different market segments. Pricing and demand are inter-related and need to be coordinated. In the hotel industry, demand for a room is cyclic in nature (day of a week, months of a year) and follows a trend (demand growth due to economic growth). These forecasts are seldom precise but provide the decision-maker with an approximate set of inputs that are used in the planning process. RM models help pinpoint demand by minimizing uncertainty and producing the best possible forecast.

Market Segment Identification

The first and foremost step in a hotel RM system is the identification of the various market segments for the hotel room, followed by implementation of a differential pricing scheme. The objective in front of the hotel is the expansion of its market and in motivating the customer to pay more than he/she will usually spend. It is further observed that customers in the business class segment are less sensitive to higher prices as opposed to those in the vacation segment. An RM system helps hotels create additional price-points by building physical and logical fences around the different market segments, as shown in the table below.

CHARACTERISTICS	HIGHER PRICE	LOWER PRICE
Physical Fences		
View	Pool view, ocean view, hill view	Non-scenic view
Size	Bigger room with more facilities and gadgets	Smaller rooms with fewer facilities
Temporal	Weekday bookings	Weekend bookings
Logical Fences		
Length of Stay	Short stay. Often one or two days	Longer stay. One night revenue can spoil three nights revenue when demand is high
Flexibility	Cancellations and rescheduling are allowed at a low penalty	High penalty for cancellation and schedule changes
Time of Purchase	Bookings are made very close to date of check-in	Bookings are made quite early
Privileges	Are rewarded loyalty privileges either as free services or free stay vouchers	No privileges
Size of Business Provided	Corporate business customers booking frequently	Self funding vacationers booking rarely
Point of Sale	Physical delivery and confirmations	By email or phone

Allocation

The next important step in a RM process is the allocation of inventory (hotel rooms) among different market segments. The ratio of discounted versus full priced rooms is not fixed during the reservation period; rather, it is "tweaked" appropriately as the date of stay approaches. The opportunity cost of selling a discounted room instead of a full priced one has to be measured in order to make the best decision. Thus, when a customer approaches the hotel for a discounted price, the manager needs to evaluate this scenario with the expected revenue from another customer who might come at a later date, willing to pay a higher price for the same room. The manager would accept the request only if the discounted price now is more than the expected price at which the room might be booked by the second customer. The key word here is "expected". RM systems use complicated mathematical algorithms to arrive at this decision using techniques such as Littlewoods and Expectation Maximization, referred to as the EM algorithm.

To explain these techniques, let us consider a simple two class scenario. A hotel has two price categories of rooms, say $60 and $100. Since the pricing is different for the two rooms, these rooms are each targeted at a different customer set. Based on the historical preference pattern of customers in each segment, it would be possible to estimate the number of customers who would be willing to buy these rooms at the given price, with a reasonable "variance". The term variance refers to a tolerance level. For example, an average 50 customers may be willing to pay $100 for some rooms, but it could also mean that the actual number of customers who turn up for the $100 room could be 60 (or even 40) with some probability, or 80 (or 30) with a lesser probability. In statistical terms, this sort of pattern for the different customer segments is said to mimic a normal distribution.

Using the past data and applying statistical know-how, we can actually estimate an "expectation" of revenue by quantifying the probability of a specific demand value and the actual revenue. In the same example, let us assume that this hotel has 100 rooms, which are similar, but priced at the time of booking. If the booking is done fairly closely to the actual date of stay, the customers may need to pay $100, whereas, they might have paid only $60 had they booked in advance. Remember that, on an average, 50 persons are willing to pay $100 for this room. Obviously, many more than 50 (say, 120) are willing to $60 for the same room. We can use the Littlewoods rule to actually estimate the number of rooms that must be protected for those customers who are willing to pay $100. If we protect too many rooms, some rooms may go vacant thereby resulting in a loss of potential revenue of at least $60 per room. On the other hand if we protect too few rooms for $100 customers, we lose the opportunity of $40 per room on that number of rooms. The Littlewoods rule guides us to arrive at an optimal number of rooms that would maximize the expectation of revenues.

Overbooking

Overbooking is the practice of intentionally selling more rooms than are available in order to offset the effect of cancellations and no-shows. Studies estimate that although a hotel is fully booked, about 5-8% of the rooms are vacant on any given date. Poor overbooking decisions can prove to be very expensive for the hotel. In the short run, it is only a loss of room revenue, but over the long-term, casualties may include decreased customer loyalty, loss of hotel reputation, etc. American Airlines developed an optimization model that maximizes net revenues associated with overbooking decisions for the airline industry.

To illustrate the overbooking model developed by the American Airlines, let us consider a B757 jet flying from Chicago to Boston. The aircraft has about 180 seats. Based on the past travel pattern, it is observed that an average of 5% (or nine passengers) do not turn up at the time of boarding the flight. If the airlines book all seats for this leg, it is likely to fly with only 171 occupied seats. However it does not mean that it never flies with 172 or more (even 180) seats occupied.

There is a lesser chance of the flight flying with 172 passengers, an even lesser chance of it flying with 175 and a miniscule chance of it flying with all 180 passengers. Therefore, if we book 181 passengers instead of 180, we are likely to end up with only 173 passengers (and almost always with lesser than 180 passengers). In an odd event of exactly 181 passengers reporting, the airline would need to bump one passenger. IATA has defined rules to compensate bumped passengers.

If we can quantify all costs (including the cost of lost goodwill), the expected revenue would be the revenue from 181 passengers minus the expected cost of compensating the one additional passenger at that odd chance. Since the probability of exactly 181 passengers turning up is so low, the revenue from that additional passenger generally compensates more than the expected cost. For this example, the optimal number of passengers that can be booked would be 186 as illustrated in the figure below.

This model can be directly applied to the hotel industry as well. The driving force behind the model is the evaluation of the trade-off between additional revenue accrued by selling an already-reserved room versus the downside from doing so. It has been found that net revenue increases with overbooking until the point where the downside from overbooking a room exceeds customer revenues. Beyond that point, the negative impact of overbooking increases rapidly because fewer and fewer customers appreciate being turned away.

Challenges

It is quite clear that while an RM system can guarantee increased revenues, it can be quite complicated to design and requires high levels of expertise for implementation. Some of the challenges facing hotels in the implementation of a robust and accurate RM system include:

- Measuring performance of an RM system is a major issue. Occupancy rates and yield are measures that are affected by external competition. An ideal measurement can be done using an opportunity model that indicates where the hotel stands in comparison to its maximum and
- Differential pricing is here to stay-customers seem resigned to the fact that hotels charge different prices for the same room. However, some customers do not like this practice and penalize the hotel by not becoming a patron. Therefore, in a fiercely competitive environment where quality of service is the key to success, RM may not work. In evaluating the efficiency of a RM system, the trade-off between generating short-term profits and creating long-term customer loyalty and "mindshare" needs to be studied carefully.
- From an operational point of view, RM can impact the motivational level of the employees. In many cases, RM takes much of the guess work out of employees, thereby reducing their decision-making responsibilities. Sometimes, employees taking reservations are paid a percentage of the sales they make, motivating them to make group bookings, which in turn may be contradictory with the objectives of an RM system.

Conclusion

As part of ongoing changes in the industry, companies throughout the entire hospitality spectrum are placing a strong emphasis on implementing major operational changes. Beyond recognizing that meaningful cost reductions must be achieved without compromising safety, capacity and service levels, they are also looking at reducing costs by increasing flexibility and improving asset utilization through an RM strategy. In doing so, they continue to reassess their true core competencies, and are looking to outsource many of these processes, as they look to optimize business efficiencies and increase profitability.

Managerial Staff of Hotels

Nature

A comfortable room, good food, and a helpful hotel staff can make being away from home an enjoyable experience for both vacationing families and business travellers. Hotel managers and assistant managers help their guests have a pleasant stay by providing many of the comforts of home, including cable television, fitness equipment, and voice mail.

Additionally, some hotels have health spas and other specialized services that the hotel manager and assistant help keep running smoothly. For business travellers, hotel managers often schedule available meeting rooms and electronic equipment, including slide projectors and fax machines.

Hotel managers are responsible for keeping the operation of their establishments efficient and profitable. In a small hotel, motel, or inn with a limited staff, the manager may oversee all aspects of operations. However, large hotels may employ hundreds of workers, and the general manager is usually aided by a number of assistant managers assigned to the various departments of the operation. In hotels of every size, managerial duties vary significantly by job title.

The general manager, for example, has overall responsibility for the operation of the hotel. Within guidelines established by the owners of the hotel or executives of the hotel chain, the general manager sets room rates, allocates funds to departments, approves expenditures, and establishes standards for service to guests, decor, housekeeping, food quality, and banquet operations. Managers who work for chains may also organize and staff a newly built hotel, refurbish an older hotel, or reorganize a hotel or motel that is not operating successfully. In order to fill some low-paying service and clerical jobs in hotels, some general managers attend career fairs. (For more information, see the statement on general managers and top executives elsewhere in the Handbook.)

Resident managers live in hotels and are on call 24 hours a day to resolve problems or emergencies. In general, though, they typically work an 8-hour day and oversee the day-to-day operations of the hotel. In many hotels, the general manager is also the resident manager.

Executive housekeepers ensure guest rooms, meeting and banquet rooms, and public areas are clean, orderly, and well maintained. They also train, schedule, and supervise the work of housekeepers, inspect rooms, and order cleaning supplies.

Front office managers coordinate reservations and room assignments as well as train and direct the hotel's front desk staff. They ensure that guests are treated courteously, complaints and problems are resolved, and requests for special services are carried out. Front office managers often have authorization to adjust charges posted on a customer's bill.

Food and beverage managers direct the food service operations of hotels. They oversee the hotels' restaurants, cocktail lounges, and banquet facilities. These managers also supervise food and beverage preparation and service workers, plan menus, set schedules, estimate costs, and deal with food suppliers. (For more information on similar workers in other industries, see the statement on restaurant and food service managers elsewhere in the Handbook.)

Convention services managers coordinate the activities of large hotels' various departments for meetings, conventions, and special events. They meet with representatives of groups or organizations to plan the number of rooms to reserve, the desired configuration of hotel meeting space, and the banquet services. During the meeting or event, they resolve unexpected problems and monitor activities to ensure that hotel operations conform to the expectations of the group.

Assistant managers help run the day-to-day operations of the hotel. In large hotels they may be responsible for activities such as personnel, accounting, office administration, marketing and sales, purchasing, security, maintenance, and pool, spa, or recreational facilities. In smaller hotels, these duties may be combined into one position. Some hotels allow an assistant manager to make decisions regarding hotel guest charges when a manager is unavailable. Computers are used extensively by hotel managers and their assistants to keep track of the guest's bill, reservations, room assignments, meetings, and special events. In addition, computers are used to order food, beverages, and supplies, as well as to prepare reports for hotel owners and top-level managers. Managers work with computer specialists to ensure that the hotel's computer system functions properly. Should the hotel's computer system fail, managers must continue to meet guests' needs.

Working Conditions

Because hotels are open around the clock, night and weekend work is common. Many hotel managers work more than 40 hours per week. Managers who live in the hotel usually have regular work schedules, but they may be called to work at any time. Some employees of resort hotels are managers during the busy season and have other duties during the rest of the year.

Hotel managers sometimes experience the pressures of coordinating a wide range of functions. Conventions and large groups of tourists may present unusual problems. Moreover, dealing with irate guests can be stressful. The job can be particularly hectic for front office managers during check-in and check-out time. Computer failures can further complicate an already busy time.

Employment

Hotel managers and assistant managers held about 76,000 jobs in 1998. Self-employed managers-primarily owners of small hotels and motels-held a significant number of these jobs. Companies that manage hotels and motels under contract employed some managers.

Training

Hotels increasingly emphasize specialized training.

Postsecondary training in hotel or restaurant management is preferred for most hotel management positions, although a college liberal arts degree may be sufficient when coupled with related hotel experience. Internships or part-time or summer work is an asset to students seeking a career in hotel management. The experience gained and the contacts made with employers can greatly benefit them after graduation. Most bachelor's degree programs include work-study opportunities.

In the past, many managers were promoted from the ranks of front desk clerks, housekeepers, waiters and chefs, and hotel sales workers. Although some employees still advance to hotel management positions without education beyond high school, postsecondary education is preferred. Restaurant management training or experience is also a good background for entering hotel management because the success of a hotel's food service and beverage operations is often of great importance to the profitability of the entire establishment.

In 1998, nearly 200 community and junior colleges and some universities offered associate, bachelor's, and graduate degree programs in hotel or restaurant management. When combined with technical institutes, vocational and trade schools, and other academic institutions, over 800 educational facilities have programs leading to formal recognition in hotel or restaurant management. Hotel management programs include instruction in hotel administration, accounting, economics, marketing, housekeeping, food service management and catering, and hotel maintenance engineering. Computer training is also an integral part of hotel management training due to the widespread use of computers in reservations, billing, and housekeeping management.

Hotel managers must be able to get along with many different people, even in stressful situations. They must be able to solve problems and concentrate on details. Initiative, self-discipline, effective communication skills, and the ability to organize and direct the work of others are also essential for managers at all levels.

Most hotels promote employees who have proven their ability and completed formal education in hotel management. Graduates of hotel or restaurant management programs usually start as trainee assistant managers. Some large hotels sponsor specialized on-the-job management training programs allowing trainees to rotate among various departments and gain a thorough knowledge of the hotel's operation. Other hotels may help finance formal training in hotel management for outstanding employees. Newly built hotels, particularly those without well-established on-the-job training programs, often prefer experienced personnel for managerial positions.

Large hotel and motel chains may offer better opportunities for advancement than small, independently owned establishments, but relocation every several years often is necessary for advancement. The large chains have more extensive career ladder programs and offer managers the opportunity to transfer to another hotel or motel in the chain or to the central office. Career advancement can be accelerated by completion of certification programs offered by the associations listed below. These programs usually require a combination of course work, examinations, and experience.

Outlook

Employment of hotel managers and assistants is expected to grow more slowly than the average for all occupations through 2008. Long hours and stressful working conditions result in high turnover in this field, so additional job openings are expected to occur as experienced managers transfer to other occupations, retire, or stop working for other reasons. Job opportunities in hotel management are expected to be especially good for persons with college degrees in hotel or restaurant management.

Increasing business travel and domestic and foreign tourism will drive employment growth of hotel managers and assistants. Managerial jobs are not expected to grow as rapidly as the hotel industry overall, however. As the industry consolidates, many chains and franchises will acquire independently owned establishments and increase the number of economy-class rooms to accommodate bargain-conscious guests. Economy hotels offer clean, comfortable rooms and front desk services without costly extras like restaurants and room service. Because there are not as many departments in these hotels, fewer managers will be needed. In addition, front desk clerks are increasingly assuming some responsibilities previously reserved for managers, further limiting the growth of managers and their assistants.

Additional demand for managers, however, is expected in suite hotels as some guests, especially business customers, are willing to pay higher prices for rooms with kitchens and suites that provide the space needed to conduct meetings. In addition to job growth in suite hotels and economy-class hotels, large full-service hotels-offering restaurants, fitness centers, large meeting rooms, and play areas for children, among other amenities-will continue to offer many trainee and managerial opportunities.

Earnings

Median annual earnings of hotel managers and assistants were $26,700 in 1998. The middle 50 percent of these workers earned between $19,820 and $34,690. The lowest 10 percent had earnings of less than $14,430, while the top 10 percent earned over $45,520. In 1997, median annual earnings in the hotel and other lodging places industry, where nearly all of these workers are employed, were $28,600. Salaries of hotel managers and assistants vary greatly according to their responsibilities and the segment of the hotel industry in which they are employed. Managers may earn bonuses up to 25 percent of their basic salary in some hotels and may also be furnished with lodging, meals, parking, laundry, and other services. In addition to typical benefits, some hotels offer profit-sharing plans and educational assistance to their employees.

7

Managing Finance in Tourism Services

There is an interrelationship between the nature or characteristics of the tourism services and the marketing mix. Hence, there is a need to take into consideration the 7 key issues while determining the criteria of the Marketing Mix (4 Ps).

The Marketing Mix

The most important factor is consumer perception of price

- o Consumer may choose not to buy when offering is perceived to be of lesser value than the asking price. Hence, bookings or visits will decline.
- o If price is low in relation to value offered, then demand will be difficult to manage and revenue loss could be substantial.

The marketer's task is to maintain a balance between; Value Perceived (Quality) & Price.

Price and Demand

- o Price has little to do with cost, and far more to do with what customer arc prepared to pay for a product.
- o How well a changed in price affect a change in total demand— price elasticity of demand.
- o In a market where the product is unique, or without satisfactory substitute, or where-the product is manufactured by a company that enjoys a monopoly or near monopoly, price will be set high.

- o In setting the prices, the company will want to know what levels of demand it is likely to experience at different prices. For a new product this is hard to gauge. The
  - two most common methods of assessing demand are:
  - Asking potential customers what they would be willing to pay for service
  - Test marketing the product at different prices in different regions.

How can price be used to control consumer demand?

- o Maximize access.
- o Restrict access.
- o Control demand in time.
- o Control demand in space.

Pricing Methods

Cost-plus Pricing

- o A standard mark-up is added to the cost of the product.
- o E.g. A bottle of wine that costs $14 may sell for $28, a 100% mark-up on cost.

Going Rate Pricing

- A strategy of going-rate pricing is the establishment of price based largely on those of competitors, with less attention paid to costs or demand.
- The firm might charge the same, more, or less than its major competitors. Some firm might charge a bit more or less, but they hold the amount of difference constant.

Skimming Pricing

- Price skimming is setting a high price when the market is price insensitive. (Higher-end market).
- To be used when:
  - o Highly differentiated product.
  - o Inelastic demand.

- o Maximize shortrun profit when product has short life cycle or demand exceeds supply over a short time period.
- o Premium product with added value.

Penetration Pricing

- o Companies set a low initial price to penetrate the market quickly and deeply, attracting many buyers and winning a large market share.
- o To be used when:
  - Little product differentiation.
  - Many competitive substitutes.
  - Inferior product.

Place

- o It is place that represents distribution of and access to the product.
- o In tourism industries, distribution systems are used to move the customer to the product: hotel, restaurant cruise ship or aeroplane.
- o Various distribution channels or intermediaries are used to market tourism services.
- o Distribution channels or Intermediaries are used to describe any dealer who acts as a link in the chain of distribution between the company and its customers.

Distribution Channel Functions

(1) *Information*-gathering and distributing marketing research and intelligence information about the marketing environment.

(2) *Promotion*-developing and spreading persuasive communication about an offer.

(3) *Contact*-finding and communicating with prospective buyers.

(4) *Matching*-shaping and fitting the offer to the buyers' needs.

(5) *Negotiation*-agreeing on price and other terms of the offer so that ownership or possession can be transferred.

(6) *Physical distribution*-transporting and storing goods.

(7) *Financing*-acquiring and using funds to cover the cost of channel work.

(8) *Risk taking*-assuming financial risks, such as the inability to sell inventory at full margin.

Why do companies choose to deal with intermediaries?

(1) It is cheaper for a company to deal through intermediaries than to set up its own network of retail shops or sell its product directly in any other way By paying a commission or other agreed form of financial remuneration to their intermediaries, companies buy the use of distributive network.

(2) The system also acts as a convenience to consumers as they can choose from a range of different products under one roof, instead of having to visit each producer's shop in turn to select their product.

(3) Through their contact, experience and specialization, intermediaries normally offer more than a firm can on its own Managing, Monitoring and Modifying Channels Channel systems will require periodic review and modification to meet changing market needs. Organizations will need to review the success of their channel systems regularly and determine is all the participants are performing at an acceptable level. It may be necessary to:

- Either expand or reduce membership at various levels or drop some existing channel members who are no longer performing.
- Change direction or consider totally new ways of looking at the business.

This is happening as the interest in call centres grows and hotels are reviewing the need for hotel representatives where call centres might be able to achieve the same results more cost effectively. Similarly, major changes are taking place in computer reservations systems with every advance in technology.

Promotion

- o Is an aspect of general marketing that promotion management deals with explicitly.
- o It includes the practices of advertising, personal selling, sales promotion, publicity and point-of-purchase communications.

Why promotional activities are carried out?

All marketing communication efforts are directed at accomplishing one or more of the following objectives:

1. Build product category wants.
2. Create brand awareness.
3. Enhance attitudes and influence intentions.
4. Facilitate purchase.
5. Promotional Mix Strategies.

Most leisure and tourism organisations use a combination of promotional activities including:

1. *Advertising:* the paid-tor sponsorship of a message in a commercially available medium. The media (press, broadcast: television and radio, posters/billboards, cinema) task is essentially to choose and buy the most economical combination of advertising space and/or time to reach defined audiences sufficiently frequently and with sufficient impact to convey the agreed messages effectively.
2. *Sales Promotion:* Those marketing activities other than personal selling and advertising and publicity that stimulate purchasing and dealer effectiveness, such as displays, shows and exhibitions, demonstrations and various non-recurrent selling efforts not in ordinary routine. Sales Promotion can be targeted at consumers, the trade and the company.
3. *Public Relations:* PR in tourism is about how people who matter to a tourism organisation think about it and how

their perceptions, attitudes and behaviour can be kept or made positive. *External PR* involves everything an organisation does that impinges on people's perceptions including: its products; its employees; its communication programmes and media coverage, its overall corporate identity; its financial reputation; its promotional activities; the buildings in which it transacts business – in short everything that contributes to the *image* of an organisation. *Internal PR* is used to build and maintain morale within an organisation through such things as good communication practices, incentive benefits, sportsman activity provision, etc.

4. *Direct Marketing:* Tourism organisations make heavy use of promotional materials mailed out or given away to customers or passed on to them by intermediaries Photographs are a crucial element of mass tour brochures. Also, maps, a critical part in tourism promotion in generating interest in a destination. One of the most difficult things to achieve in brochures aimed at the mass market is competitive differentiation.
5. *Personal Selling:* An interpersonal process whereby the seller ascertains, activates and satisfies the needs and wants of the buyer so that both the seller and buyer benefits. It is a method of influencing the purchase. The selling sequence include prospecting and qualifying, planning and delivering sales presentations, overcoming objections and closing the sale.

Product

Problems in Managing Services

The effectiveness of planning the marketing mix depends as much on the ability to select the right target market as on the skill in devising a product which will generate high levels of satisfaction. Hence, the decision depends very much on the capability of the marketers to tackle the following issues concerning tourism services:

Intangible Nature of Business

Customer cannot physically evaluate or sample most services: they tend to rely on other people's experiences with these services Customers place great value on the advice of hospitality and travel experts, such as travel agents Implications:

- o Tourism marketers tend to 'tangibilize' the tourism offering in brochures and videos-visual displays of the real thing.
- o Marketers tend to generate positive "word-of-mouth" among the customers.

Variability in Production Methods

Quality control of services is neither as precise nor as easy to achieve because of the human factors that are involved in supplying them All staff members cannot consistently provide the same level of service as their colleagues

- * Although standardised service is an admirable target that all organisations should try to achieve it is unrealistic.
- * The same standardisation cannot be provided since the actions of service staff, other+customers and the customers themselves make the experience more variable.
- * Hotels, restaurants, airlines, theme parks and travel agencies are some of the 'factories' in the business. Behaviour of one customer can ruin the service experience of others.
- * Implications:
  - o Tourism marketer design processes to minimise differences in service encounters and provision between different outlets or between different shifts at a hotel. Example: Provision of uniforms and of similar physical surroundings illustrates evidence of standardisation.

Perishability

- * Service is highly perishable-"like a running tap in a sink with no plug".

* An unoccupied seat on a train or bed in a guesthouse is lost forever.
* Services and the time available to experience them cannot be stored.
* Implications:
    - o The management task emphasises managing demand and capacity to a degree of time tuning. Example: Airlines offer stand by fares to those willing to fill unexpected empty seats at short notice.

Distribution Channels

There is no physical distribution system in tourism industry. Instead, there are many intermediaries in the hospitality and travel industry where the items are being purchased.

Cost Determination

Services are both variable and intangible. Some customers might require more attention than others.

Relationship of Services to Providers

* Some services are inseparable from the individuals who provide them.
* Example: Restaurant-whose chefs or owners have developed unique reputations for their food, personalities or both.
* Implications:
    - o Marketers attempt to devise delivery systems which ease interaction and invest in campaigns to educate staff and consumers as to how to get the best from the interaction.
    - o Training in hotels emphasises how staff can manage the interaction.

Target Marketing

- o In tourism industry, we need to acknowledge that not all individuals would want to buy from us.

- ;e might not have the services that they may be looking for.
- And hence, it is important to consider targeting the right market to ensure success of our business.
- Marketing is about developing the right product/service to the right market/people so that they will be satisfied with what they receive.
- Target marketing can be defined as:
  - Seller identifies market segments (groups), selects one or more and develops products and marketing mixes tailored to each selected segments.

Market Segmention

- Involves dividing market into distinct groups of buyers who requires different products or marketing mixes.
- There is no single way to segment a market
- MaNor variables include.
  - (a) Geographic Segmentation divide market according to location e.g. nations, regions, states, countries, cities.
  - (b) Demographic Segmentation divide market into groups, based on demographic variables e.g. age, gender, family life cycle, income, occupation, education, religion, race/culture, nationality.
  - (c) psychographic Segmentation divide buyers into different groups, based on social class, lifestyle, and personality characteristics.
  - (d) Behaviour Segmentation buyer is divided into groups, based on knowledge, attitude, usage rate, and response.

Refers to the buying behaviour of final customers (individuals and households) to buy goods and services for personal consumption MaNor factors influencing buying behaviour include.

E Ypxyvi Jegxsvw

Culture comprise of the basic values, perceptions, want and behaviour that a person learns continuously in a society Culture is expressed through tangible items such as food, buildings, clothing and art. e.g. the culture shift toward greater concern about health and fitness has resulted in many hotels adding exercise rooms/ health clubs. e.g. KFC, piazza and Burger King in Israel adapted their menus to make them kosher for Passover (.ewish) Subculture groups of population with shared value system base oncommon experiences and situations Social classesare relatively permanent and ordered divisions in a society whose members share similar values, interests and behaviours e.g. income, occupation, education, wealth Social classes show distinct product and brand preferences in such areas as food, travel and leisure activity. e.g. CE3, managers and directors organizations often indulge in golfing activities.

Reference Group

A personvs refer group consists of all the groups that have a direct/indirect influence on the personvs attitude/behaviour e.g. artist, idol Family Marketers have examined the role and influence of the husband, wife and children on the purchase of different products and services.

Roles and Status: A person position in each group can be defined in terms of role and status a role consists of the activities that a person is expected to perform each role carried a status e.g. pinna parents daughter Family wife/mother Company staff.

B9=ER DECISI32 4R3CESS

This model emphasizes that the buying process starts long before and continues long after the actual purchases It encourages marketer to focus on the entire buying process rather than Nust the purchasing decision.

Problem Recognition

The buying process starts when the buyer recognizes a problem or need.

The need can be triggered by internal and external stimuli. They should research customers to find out what kinds of needs/ problems, led them to purchase an items, what brought these needs about, and how they led consumers to choose a particular product. E.g. SPA Travel relaxation/need to get out of city life.

Information Search

1. The strength of drive.
2. The amount of initial information.
3. The ease of obtaining the information.
4. The value placed on additional information.
5. The satisfaction one gets from search.

Consumer can obtain information from several sources personal sources family, friends, neighbours, acquaintances Commercial sources z sales person, packaging, advertising, dealers, displays public sources z restaurant reviews, editorials in the travel section Therefore, a company must design its marketing mix to make prospects aware of and knowledgeable about the features and benefits of its products/brands.

E.g. TRA:E0 Fair

(1) promote in newspaper (create awareness).

(2) initial information (from newspaper or a call to travel agent).

(3) obtain information from internet, visit travel agents.

(4) value (are the information of high quality trustworthy).

(5) satisfaction (are consumers happy with the search).

Evaluation of Alternatives

- This is the stage where consumer makes an assessment of the goods/services offered and is considering the alternatives.
- The marketer must ensure that his product/service is on the list of alternatives.
- The buyer must be convinced of its suitability before the buyer can proceed to the buying/purchase decision.
- The product/service must be readily available to the consumer.

Purchase Decision

- The buyer would have made a decision by now as to which product/service is suitable to fulfil his/her needs.

- o The ideal product would have all the attributes/ characteristics that the customer is looking for:
  - Then the decision to purchase is made, the product that is thought to be most suitable will be selected.
  - However, 2 factors can influence the purchase intention and the purchase decision.
    - (i) Attitudes of others (getting information from relatives/family members).
    - (ii) Unexpected situational factors (e.g. earthquakes, flood, SARS, effect of tsunami).

Post Purchase Behaviour

- o Feelings felt by the buyer towards the product offer that has been purchased.
- o To avoid post purchase dissonance, there must be no gap between the expectations of the buyer and the actual product performance.
- o The buyervs decision to buy the product again later will depend on the buyervs satisfaction with the product performance.

Paper on Community Travel and Tourism Marketing

Every community if affected by visitors. While many communities recognize opportunities for growth in the tourism industry, options at the local level expand when travellers are included. Travellers are people away from home temporarily. In collecting data, sometimes "more than miles away from home" further defines a traveller.

This travel may result from a variety of sources: a pleasure vacation, business and convention purposes, friends and relatives, special events and festivals, sport recreation, historic sites, specific attractions, or when people pass-through headed for another destination. The cash register doesn't sort out travel purchases this way, and in reality it is impractical to separate tourists from travellers. All visitors are important to the travel and tourism industry.

Minnesota is experiencing a boom in communities organizing to attract and host visitors as a way to diversify and boost economies. The impact of travel and tourism on the local economy goes beyond first level expenditures at food, lodging, gas, entertainment, and retail establishments. Travel spending brings in outside dollars that "turn over" in the community. Even if you do not have direct contact with travellers, the money filters through the entire economy as residents re-spend travel dollars. But the increased interest in tourism translates to fierce competition in the marketplace.

Key to gaining the attention of potential tourists is development of a community marketing, not a selling approach. Marketing is a continuous, coördinated set of activities associated with efficiently distributing products to high potential markets. It involves making decisions about product, price, promotion, and distribution. Marketing focuses on providing customer benefits and satisfying needs better than the competition. It is based on the principle that consumer buying resistance will be overcome if the product satisfies buyer needs.

In contrast, selling focuses on the product offered rather than satisfying customer needs. It assumes that the main thing necessary to sell the product is to overcome purchase resistance. A statement reflecting the selling approach is "we will attract tourists to Our City because we want tourists and everyone would want to visit. Selling is only a small part of marketing. The formal marketing process involves six steps:

- Analyse your current situation.
- Identify product(s).
- Select target market(s).
- Set objectives.
- Carry out promotion strategies.
- Evaluate results.

When the structure to support tourism is in place-1) attractions, 2) services and facilities, 3) an information/direction/interpretive system, and 4) transportation linkages-communities can move to market their unique tourist and travel experiences. This publication outlines one approach for preparing a marketing that describes how you will get visitors to stop, to stay, to tell others, and to return.

Analyse your Current Situation

What does your community have that travellers want? The first step in the marketing process is to conduct an inventory and analysis of the travel and tourism industry and its potential within your area. Tourism isn't just a community or collection of small businesses with an interest in attracting visitors. Tourism is an entire "region" organizing to draw and host travellers-it's an overall view with a wide angle lens. Analysis answers the question "what is?" As a basis for "what could be?" Ten crucial questions for a community to answer on a regular basis include:

1. What attractions exist that will entice people to stop and visit?
2. What hospitality services and facilities are available?
3. What experiences are visitors having in the community?
4. What promotion methods are used? How well do they work?
5. What are the current markets?
6. What is the competition for your community?
7. How is tourism related to the community lifestyle and goals?"
8. What roles do community organizations play in tourism development?
9. What are trends that affect the tourism industry?
10. What are the community strengths and weaknesses, problems and opportunities in serving visitors?

Attractions (Question 1)

Through fate or creativity, most communities have tourist attractions that draw visitors. A community's basic assets may include:

- Natural resources, or a scenic setting;
- Human-made attractions such as racetracks, museums, or resorts;
- Historical sites;
- Cultural and ethnic resources;
- Recreation opportunities;
- Special events and festivals;
- Availability of high quality personal services such as shopping, medical care and education; or
- Local industries and economic base.

Describe each attraction, including quality. How many of each type of attraction are there? Look forward and list potential visitor resources that could be enhanced or used more fully. The Minnesota Extension Service publication "So Community Wants Tourism" outlines the range of travel attractors that determine a community's capability to bring travellers.

As you develop a community tourism campaign, it is useful to separate "core" attractions that are a prime reason for travel, from secondary "supporting" attractions that enhance a visitor's experience once they are there. There are infinite reasons to visit Minneapolis and St. Paul, but Twin Cities Attractions Council is organized to promote the plus theatres, museums, special events, and other core attractions that draw large audiences. This distinction is useful when you are selecting an image for your marketing program.

The Spicer area tourism committee has developed a four-tier list of tourism assets: most important (includes Green Lake, resorts, 2 hours to Twin Cities); important (Sibley State Park, fishing, golf course); significant (fall colours, hunting, July 4 celebration); and contributing (antique shops, sailing regattas, farm tours). Spicer's marketing theme reflects this ranking.

Hospitality Services (Question 2)

The economic impact of tourism largely comes from spending in the hospitality sector primarily composed of private commercial businesses. The U.S. Travel Data Centre estimates tourist dollar expenditures on a state wide basis by category (1985):

* Food $0.26,
* Public transportation.25,
* Auto transportation.17,
* Lodging.15,
* Entertainment & recreation.09,
* Retail and other.08,
* $1.00.

It is useful to have local or regional expenditure data to track the travel industry and develop public support for this economic sector. However, data collection requires a visitor survey, and study and questionnaire design are complex. Seek assistance from industry professionals in developing a data base that accurately represents spending patterns.

Good restaurants and sufficient overnight lodging capacity are essential. Describe the mix of establishments, their occupancy, and their services. For example, do motels have facilities for families such as pools and playgrounds, or are they positioned to attract business meetings where evening entertainment may be a factor in the decision to make reservations? Grocery stores, specialty retail shops, entertainment and service stations also support the visitor industry.

Questions about the adequacy of public services come into play. Transportation issues such as roadway congestion, parking and signing, restroom availability, and utilities (sewage and trash disposal) assume importance as the industry expands. Plans for a proposed megamall in the Twin include construction to widen roads in the area.

Tourism Today (Questions 3, 4, and 5)

The tourism experience your community promotes now, whether or accidental, is generally a good indicator for the future. It is often easier to modify and market a travel experience that has evolved over time and is built on local flavour, than Do introduce and develop a new form of tourism that does not match local culture, environment, and heritage. Mississippi Rivertown Rendezvous, an organization promoting the towns along the river corridor from Hastings to Winona, builds upon a common heritage and landscape.

Describe the visitor experience your community offers both in terms of tangibles: the resorts, the boating, the location, as well as the intangibles. Talk about customer benefits when you think about intangibles: rest and relaxation, friendliness, excitement. Then outline and valuate promotion strategies now in use to envision future options. Through survey or observation, determine who is buying your community's experience now. Customers who have visited (even though there may have been no major promotion campaign) are a good clue about the target market your community naturally appeals to.

Outside Influences (Questions 6 through 9)

Tourism marketing occurs within a competitive marketplace that goes well beyond the community boundaries. There are many forms of competition for your customers and their dollars-but neighbouring communities generally are not one of them. A number of strong travel-oriented communities, working together on regional promotion, results in a stronger destination image, a greater variety of attractions and facilities, wider market exposure, and a healthy degree of competition that spurs improvements. The Land of Legends group-a ring of communities within 60 miles of Itasca State Park could not promote itself as a major destination without the involvement of many Chambers of Commerce. This "critical mass" of diverse attractions and quality services also enables the Land of Legends area to attract and host "fam" (familiarization) tours for travel writers and tour brokers as part of an overall marketing program.

More important, there is competition for how consumers spend their discretionary dollar. The purchase of a VCR, buying a more expensive car, or saving for a college education means less money is available for leisure and travel. You also have to be concerned with other destination areas on a national level. Consumers have worldwide choices today; you must understand your competition and their strategies to market your competitive advantages.

In promoting certain visitor experiences, assess what type of tourism is compatible with local lifestyles. For example, many residents of northwestern Minnesota enjoy the hunting opportunities. They use the same resource nonlocal hunters use. Conflicts over resource use must be negotiated before hunting is promoted as a primary visitor attraction. In other areas, emphasis on scattered small town activities is more appropriate than major new construction and facility development. The latest brochure for Southeastern Minnesota Historic Bluff Country emphasizes small-scale tourism businesses such as canoe rental, locally made arts and crafts, bed and breakfasts, and a lefsa factory tour. It is a format designed to encourage travellers to wander and explore the area, rather than directing everyone to a few major sites. In addition, specify the roles various community organizations play in development and promotion, and understand social trends that influence your market position. React quickly when they occur. For example, the move toward shorter getaway mini-vacations is radically changing travel industry strategies.

Where are We Now? (Question 10)

Summarize findings on community attractions, services and facilities, the current travel industry and outside influences in a Written summary statement. Combine relevant in an outline of community strengths and weaknesses, problem opportunities for tourism. Spend sufficient time on this step: analysis is the basis for subsequent decisions about marketing your community's unique visitor experiences.

Identify Product

What is your community marketing? One main reason people travel is to experience a new and different environment. After the situation analysis, most communities find they are faced with multiple options for attracting tourists. The challenge is to choose one dominant identity among all these alternatives. You can not and should not promote all of the community attributes equally. In a tourism marketplace where consumers are faced with diverse choices, need an "edge" to set yourself apart from the competition. You need to create a unique product with a theme or identity that characterizes major promotion efforts. Red Lake Riverlands-Red Lake Falls, Thief River Falls, Crookston, East Grand Forks-features river uses like tubing and boat tours, and nearby food and lodging services.

The thirteen Iron Trail United Communities capitalize on the unique mining characteristics and strong ethnic heritage of the Range. Iron world, with its train and festival series, Hill Annex Mine and Tower-Soudan State Park are the core attractions that support the mining theme. A region-wide visitor newspaper and radio information network are part of this cooperative marketing approach.

An example from the private sector is three ski resorts that offer the same hills, the same snow, and the same lift equipment. One business bills itself as a "mountain of hospitality," another is a family resort and the third sells serious, technical skiing.

A marketing theme is the one main idea or message you want to communicate. It should be based on satisfying visitor needs. Theme development requires creativity, and there are advertising agencies that specialize in "positioning" a product in the marketplace and developing a parallel marketing campaign. Consult the Minnesota Extension Service sheet "Creating a Tourism Promotional Theme.

Select Target Markets

Who will buy the product your community is marketing? One certain way to fail is to try to please everyone. A target market is a group of individuals sharing common characteristics, toward whom marketing efforts will be directed. The process of dividing the total market into high-potential target markets is called market segmentation and involves these steps:

- Identifying and describing the different segments that make up the total market;
- Evaluating the economic potential of each segment;
- Choosing one or more market segments on which to focus.

Current visitors are a good indication of target markets attracted to your community. New prospects are likely to have many of the same characteristics unless you are planning a product shift. Target markets can be defined by several factors: geography, demographics, and behaviour.

Geography refers to potential visitors: where they live and they travel. Negative travel time and positive attraction factors are recognized widely as the two main variables that determine what customers choose to see and where they choose to go. Travel time and distance can be negative factors for potential visitors, but the power of an area's tourist attractions may be a counteracting positive factor. A destination that offers a large variety of interesting attractions has more pull, at an equal distance, than a location that offers only one or a few low interest attractions. This doesn't cancel the fact that travel to and from an area is an important part of the total experience, as "pass-through" communities have discovered. Demographics refers to characteristics like age, sex, marital status, number and ages of children and life stage (young single adult or retired) that have direct and obvious effects on travel patterns. For example, unmarried men and married couples with young children have vastly different spending patterns. Behaviour refers to how potential tourists act, such as length of stay, new us. Repeat visitors, and skills (novice expert). But market segmentation using behaviour variables also refers to why they behave as they do, their interests, and their values. There are many factors that affect travel by individual consumers: the reasons for travel, activities enjoyed during travel, a person's general interests and opinions about travel, and personal values.

For one person, travel may mean a tour of museums, monuments and other cultural attractions. Another person may travel to a meeting of a professional organization. A third person seeks amusement at a sporting event; another visits a park to fish. For different reasons they engage in different activities while travelling and value different types of attractions.

Information on behaviour can be difficult and expensive to collect. Some details are available from observing visitors analysing existing records, but most knowledge is likely to come from surveys or interviews. Work with a marketing professional about survey design to assure a representative sample if you try this method.

New and even established host communities must evaluate each major target market for its economic potential. Consider your product and estimate the drawing power of the attractions. Think about proximity to metropolitan areas and the quality of the transportation network. Consider the of people travelling near your area; consult Minnesota Department of Transportation records.

Use size and accessibility of the target market as criteria. There must be enough members of the target market justify the investment in reaching them. You must be able to reach the target market through a standard form of promotion. Boaters, runners, and anglers, for example, are very accessible: they belong to organizations and read specialized publications. In contrast, young single parents less accessible market because there is no common affiliation or central source of information.

Finally, select one or more of the target markets. You can concentrate on a single target market to the exclusion of all others, or you can use a strategy where promotion campaigns are developed for two or more markets simultaneously. It is likely you will change market segments during the season in the same way resort operators shift their marketing efforts from anglers (spring) to families (summer) to retired couples (fall). Most important, a community shouldn't try to be all things to all consumers. Primary destination areas like the Twin Cities, state offices of tourism, and major attractions such as Disneyland have the resources to accomplish that. You are much more likely to be successful if you narrow down the target market you want to reach.

Set Marketing Objectives

Now write down marketing objectives that clearly state what community wants to accomplish in its promotion campaign. Objectives keep energy and action focused on what's important. They help you track your success and judge when it is time to review and shift strategies. A good objective contains four elements:

- A specific action of interest such as increased visitation, sales volume, or awareness;
- A measurable outcome, expressed in dollars, a percentage or numbers for example, that indicates how much change will
- A time frame within which the action should occur; and
- An indication of the target market you are trying to reach. Some poorly stated objectives are "to increase visits," "to midweek business," and "to attract more retired couples." In contrast, some examples of well-written objectives follow:
- In the next year, increase midweek (Monday-Thursday) occupancy to 55 percent by attracting business travellers.
- The Chamber of Commerce will book 500 advance reservations from vacationers travelling the Lake Superior circle route in summer (June 1 through Labour Day).
- Increase phone and mail inquiries by 20 percent from fall magazine advertising between August 15 and October 15.
- Increase retail sales on main street during a summer festival by 25 percent over last year's.

Carry out Promotion Strategies

Many communities and private entrepreneurs mistakenly assume that marketing is just deciding on a promotion strategy. They direct broad appeals to poorly defined markets through a variety of media. You can't afford to spend scarce promotion dollars in appealing to people who are not prospects for purchase of your product. Effective and efficient promotion decisions build from a situation analysis, identifying products, selecting target markets and setting objectives.

The message content comes directly from the product and the associated theme. It emphasizes both tangible and intangible aspects, focusing on customer benefits your product offers.

Carrying out promotion strategies involves taking your message to the consumer through a specific delivery system.

Promotion is any attempt to stimulate sales by persuasive or informative communications to current or potential customers. The major types of promotion used to stimulate travel and tourism follow:

Advertising: Any paid form of nonpersonal presentation and promotion of ideas, goods, or services by an identified sponsor using mass media. Television, radio and print media some of the major Minnesota destinations are an example.

Personal Selling: An oral or written presentation to one or prospective customers on a face-to-face basis, including telephone solicitation and direct mail. Attendance at sports shows is a form of personal selling.

Sales Promotions: Activities other than advertising and personal selling that stimulate purchasing or create awareness. Sales promotions, including contests featuring free tickets or trips, may be geared toward the individual visitor, while other promotions may be directed toward organizations selling travel services. The Duluth contest to guess the date the first ship will enter the harbour in spring is an example.

Public Relations: A nonpaid presentation of ideas, goods or services generally using mass media. Unlike advertising there is no identifying sponsor. Travel feature stories written after a "fam" (familiarization) tour are a result of public relations efforts.

These promotional categories are known together as the promotional mix. Strictly speaking, the promotional mix refers to the relative amounts of efforts or dollars put into each major promotional category. To find its optimal tourism promotional mix, your community might look at towns comparable size and attracting power. However, do not copy programs-no two communities will be exactly alike.

Finally, the committee may be drawn from owners. The committee structure is used most often to guide tourism development.

There are several ways to organize a tourism promotion committee. Some groups originate within the Chamber of

Commerce because of shared goals. Others form freestanding community endeavour; the final plan must represent goals independent committees with community-wide representation.

The Minnesota Extension Service publication "Tourism Advertising: Some Basics" outlines a process for selecting an advertising strategy. The tools discussed include magazines, newspapers, radio, television, direct mail, and outdoor displays.

Evaluate Results

There is no secret promotional formula. Test and evaluate regularly. A community or business must continually monitor evaluate results, and experiment with various types of promotion. Even with an effective promotional mix now, the situation may change. Preferences and characteristics of travellers change: marketing efforts must respond.

Evaluate Results

The Minnesota Extension Service publication "Evaluating Tourism Advertising with Cost-Comparison Methods" describes methods such as cost per inquiry, cost per reservation, and return on investment. The importance of coding advertisements to track results cannot be overemphasized.

The Next Step

Working through the tourism development process is a community endeavour; the final plan must represent goals commonly agreed to by area residents and business owners. The committee is used most often to guide tourism development.

There are several ways to organize a tourism promotion committee. Some groups originate within the Chamber of Commerce because of shared goals. Others form freestanding independent committees with community-wide representation.

Finally, the committee may be drawn from current leaders in existing tourism agencies, associations, businesses, and attractions. You know the dynamics of your community best to pull together a core group of individuals make things happen. There must be periodic feedback between the committee and the community at large. In some locations, the tourism committee begins its task with a community-wide survey (by mail, newspaper, or phone) to solicit opinions about tourism development. The results advise the committee and can create a widespread base of public support early in the process. The other strategy is to be sure there is always an opportunity for community discussion at key decision points. The local media can play a major role in keeping the public informed.

Here are seven steps to get started (from "Developing a Tourism Organization," 1987, a Michigan State University Extension Service booklet):

1. Select a name that creates an image and identifies the group.
2. Develop a policy statement, including a statement of purpose and bylaws.
3. Develop an action program: set goals and methods of accomplishing them.
4. Set up committees and subcommittees as needed. Some of the major tasks relate to community involvement, attractions and support services, promotion, budgets, research, and information.
5. Create community awareness and support for tourism.
6. Establish lines of communication and develop a flow of information.
7. Foster a spirit of close cooperation and coordination among the various communities, agencies, and other organizations.

Where to Look for Funding

Often good community marketing plans go unrealized or even unused because financial support could not be obtained. Funding can be a difficult obstacle. Communities that have developed a steady and reliable source of marketing funds generally have the most success. Constant scrambling for marketing funds drains energy away from the original marketing objectives. Some of the basic strategies used to raise money for tourism and travel marketing are a lodging tax, local government sources, internal organizational fundraising, private businesses, foundations, and the Minnesota Office of Tourism. Adapt these standard methods to your local situation. Minnesota Statutes permit the creation of a local option lodging tax. Home rule or statutory cities and townships with elected officials may enact a tax of up to three percent on the proceeds of a lodging facility-with a possible extension to municipal campgrounds. In unorganized townships, county officials may enact a lodging tax. Cities townships can create joint districts to better reflect the local tourism region.

Of the proceeds collected, 95 percent must be used to fund marketing and promotion of the area as a tourism or convention destination. These monies may not be used for capital expenditures such as buildings, parks, and civic centres. Lodging facilities are directly affected by the tax, so any plans for a lodging tax should include early discussions with representatives of overnight accommodations. Some communities have had special legislation passed to help fund tourism programs: two options are expansion of the tax base or increases in the tax ceiling. It is normally difficult to pass special interest legislation, but such authority can prove valuable to communities where tourism is a major industry.

Many local governments recognize the importance of the tourism and travel industry to their economies; a number of provide funding to marketing programs implemented by local groups. Monies can come from the general fund, bonding sources, special assessments, or a variety of other sources. Government support can greatly assist local marketing efforts, but funding is less stable due to changing demands for government funds, the health of the local economy, and the fortunes of local politicians.

Tourism organizations typically employ some internal fundraising strategies, in addition to outside sources. Membership dues is the most common method. Set either a standard rate or variable fees based on factors such as business size or number of employees. The organization's ability to attract members then becomes critical. Assessments above and beyond dues are another alternative. Assessments are often based on percent of gross revenue or business size. These may help to fund an overall marketing program, but are also used to pay for specific promotional efforts. Tourism organizations can also sell products, services, and activities directly to the public for income.

Examples are publications, souvenirs and merchandise, tours and tour guides, and operation of attractions, special events, festivals or auctions. Major businesses operating in the community and benefitting from travel and tourism sometimes make substantial contributions to a marketing program. An important element in obtaining this support is to thoroughly identify the benefits of such a contribution, both to the marketing program and the contributor. Direct benefits-increased sales-as well as secondary benefits-general expansion of the local economy-are important. Tax benefits may be an issue. Do not overlook the potential to build goodwill in the community.

There are opportunities to obtain project-specific grants through organizations such as foundations, the Minnesota Office of Tourism and nonlocal private businesses that will fund ongoing expenses for tourism marketing. Projects that provide promotion to an expanded region or attempt to market an area with an innovative approach are more likely to attract a foundation grant. The Minnesota Office of Tourism administers a joint venture marketing program that allocates matching funds on a competitive basis for advertising, creative marketing, and new brochure development. Private businesses beyond the specific area might also sponsor an activity if there is a connection between their product and the focus of the event. For example, dog food manufacturers could be approached for national sponsorship of a sled dog race.

Travel and Tourism Resources

Tourism USA: Guidelines for Tourism Development. 1986. University of Missouri, Dept. of Recreation and Park Administration, University Extension. Prepared for the U.S. of Commerce.

- Excellent "how to" handbook with sections on) appraising potential; 2) planning for tourism; 3) assessing product and market; 4) marketing tourism; visitor services; sources of assistance. Single copies are available for $3.00 from U.S. Dept. of Commerce, 1 4th & Constitution, Room 1 865, Washington, D.C. 20030, 202-377-0140. Managing Small Resorts for Profit. 1 985. Minnesota Extension Service, University of Minnesota.

- Contains a marketing section with articles on the market planning process, brochure development, advertising, positioning and package tours. Available for $20.00 from Bud Crewdson, Small Business Development Centre, Minnesota Extension Service, 248 Classroom Office Building, University of Minnesota, St. Paul, MN 551 08, 61 2-625-31 Minnesota Office of Tourism, 250 Skyway Level, 375 Jackson Street, St. Paul, MN 551 0 1,-800-652-9141, 6 1 2-296-Contact for information on a joint venture marketing program. Marketing activities may be eligible for matching funds allocated on a competitive basis to any local, regional, or statewide nonprofit organization formed to promote tourism. Tourism Centre, Minnesota Extension Service, University of Minnesota, 240 Coffey Hall, 1420 Eckles Avenue, St. Paul, MN 55108.
- Offers educational programs and materials for the visitor industry on community tourism development and small business management. Contact your local county extension agent for copies of the extension publications listed in the folder. So Your Community Wants Tourism: Guidelines for Developing Income from Tourism in Your Community (CD-FO-0679, Available 1988) Creating a Tourism Promotional Theme Tourism Advertising: Some Basics (CD-FO-331 1) "Evaluating Tourism Advertising with Cost Comparison Methods" (CD-FO-3372) Tourism Brochures to Boost Business (CD-FO-3273).

Community Improvement Resources

Tourism development depends on citizen cooperation to accomplish community goals and improve the local environment. The Minnesota Department of Trade and Economic development administers four such programs that give residents an opportunity to develop expertise in identifying and using community resources-the Minnesota Community Improvement Program, the Governor's Design Team, Minnesota Main Street, and Minnesota Beautiful. Program coordinators can be reached at the Department of Trade and Economic Development, 900 American Centre Building, 1 50 East Kellogg Blvd., St. Paul, MN 551 01. The general office number is 612-297-3190.

The Minnesota Community Improvement Program (MCIP) is a community (or county) revitalization and recognition program. Citizens conduct a community analysis and set goals. They build broad support networks and document the improvement process so that MCIP judges can evaluate annual progress. The Minnesota Extension Service provides educational and technical support. Involvement in MCIP can build the skills and coalitions necessary to accomplish other specific tasks such as economic development, downtown revitalization and design, and beautification.

The Governor's Design Team calls on architects, landscape designers, urban planners, artists, and other professionals volunteer their time and services and virtually descend on a community for a two-to three-day intensive design consultation and work session. Communities want the team to a fresh look and new ideas in such areas a downtown revitalized town image, and development potential. Before applying for a visit, the community should focus on specific issues and areas of need. During a visit, broad-based active citizen support and involvement is expected.

Minnesota Main Street encourages revitalization of downtowns in small and midsize cities, working with assets already inherent in the downtown tradition. Rebuilding main street's image depends on improvements in organization, promotion, design, and economic restructuring, made in operation with downtown groups.

Minnesota Beautiful supports activities that help keep Minnesota a clean and quality place to live, work, and visit. Projects include recycling, landscaping, general cleanup of waste materials and unsightly areas, tree planting, and mineland reclamation. Minnesota Beautiful offers educational materials to communities undertaking these projects, and organizes an annual conference to recognize significant progress.

Cultural Tourism Promotion and Policy in Malaysia

Malaysia is experiencing a tremendous pace of tourism development. Tourism sector has been recognized by Malaysian government as a major source of revenue and catalyst to the Malaysian economic renaissance. Tourist arrivals to Malaysia for the last ten years have shown a significant rise. In the year 2004, this country attracted 15.7 million foreign tourists generating around RM29.7 billion into the company. Major tourist market for Malaysia has been the neighbouring ASEAN nations especially Singapore, Thailand, Indonesia and Brunei. Other main traditional foreign markets include China, Japan, Taiwan and India.

Table 1: Tourist arrivals and receipts to Malaysia

Year	*Arrivals (million)*	*Receipts (RM millions)*
1995	7.46	9,174.9
1996	7.14	10,354.1
1997	6.21	9,699.6
1998	5.55	8,580.4
1999	7.93	12,321.3
2000	10.22	17,335.4
2001	12.78	24,221.5
2002	13.29	25,781.1
2003	10.58	21,291.1
2004	15.70	29,651.4

Source: Tourism Malaysia, 2005

Coupled with the growth in tourism is a booming interest in the 'new tourism'. Cultural tourism has emerged as a potential form of alternative tourism among both international tourists as well as Malaysian domestic travellers. Cultural tourism in Malaysia attracted great publicities with the increase in the number of incoming tourists annually. Malaysia has marvelous cultural tourism resources that are readily available to be explored such as the existence of multicultural, historical buildings, colorful lifestyles and friendly atmosphere. The purpose of this paper is to give an overview of the promotion of culture and heritage in Malaysia as well as the related strategies and policies that support the measure. It also discusses several underlying issues pertaining the cultural management in Malaysia.

Defining Cultural Tourism

Culture in tourism is an important issue. The relationship between tourism and culture can take many forms and the outcome can be viewed as negative and positive when meeting of hosts and visitors occurs and possibly leads to the transformation of the hosts' culture. The destruction of local culture as a result of tourism is well documented.

However, studies by researchers' consider this as a lopsided view of the impact of tourism. Studies have shown that tourism have lead to the strengthening of local culture. Culture is defined broadly as quoted in Meethan (2001:117), *".....as a set of practices, based on forms of knowledge, which encapsulate common values and act as general guiding principles. It is through these forms of knowledge that distinctions are created and maintained, so that, for example, one culture is marked off as different from another".*

World Tourism Organization (1985) defines cultural tourism as the movements of persons for essentially cultural motivations such as study tours, performing arts and cultural tours; travel to festivals and other related events. Essentially, cultural tourism is based on the mosaic of places, traditions, art forms, celebrations and experiences that portray ones nation and its people.

Meethan (2001:128) rightly observed that there are array of tourist activities that come under the heading of cultural tourism. However, he argues for a distinct demarcation of cultural tourism and hence a distinct profile of cultural tourists quotes;

> *"....the cultural tourists are those who go about their leisure in a more serious frame of mind. To be a cultural*

> *tourist.....is to go beyond idle leisure and to return enriched with knowledge of other places and other people even if this involves 'gazing' at or collecting in some way, the commodation essences of otherness".*

Studies of western culture by Richard (1994) described the cultural tourists were *'a high socioeconomic status, high level of educational attainment, adequate leisure time, and often having occupations related to the culture industries'.* It must be borne in mind that culture is not static but one that is dynamic and evolving. Meethan (2001: 127) draw attention to globalization of culture and also the mobilization of culture for internal and external purposes. Yamashita, Kadir and Eades (1997: 29-30) further illustrates the processes that transform culture.

Heritage tourism can be classified as a subclass of cultural tourism. Both cultural and heritage tourism become a growing segment of the tourism marketplace. Cultural tourists appear to be motivated for different reasons than do traditional tourists. Some tourism destinations see cultural tourism as a promotion for tourism products, and this has been lamented. Millar (1989) and others suggest that heritage tourism is "about the cultural traditions, places and values that... groups throughout the world are proud to conserve." Cultural traditions such as family patterns, religious practices, folklore traditions, and social customs attract individuals interested in heritage as do monuments, museums, battlefields, historic structures, and landmarks.

Cultural Tourism in Malaysia and its Management

In Malaysia, heritage and culture has also been identified as new niche products to be developed extensively in tourism development. Cultural vibrancy is clearly manifested in the ongoing and successful "Malaysia: Truly Asia" promotional drive by the country's promotion arm, Tourism Malaysia. In this promotion, Malaysia boasts to host a wide variety of Asian ethnic groups that making it into a little Asia. Malaysia also has distinctive multicultural architectural heritage with strong Islamic, Chinese and Western influences; all of which have been portrayed in the heritage buildings.

The major heritage elements; historic building, historical sites and unique local cultures are commonly found in many historic cities throughout Malaysia. An inventory has revealed that 30,000 heritage buildings are located in 162 cities throughout Malaysia. From this figure, 69.6% are shop houses and dwellings built before World War II. The unique colonial architectural styles of buildings have played major role in the creation of historic cities such as George Town, Ipoh, Malacca, Tapping, Koala Lumpur and Kuching.

Table 2 Distributions of Pre-War Buildings in Selected States in Malaysia

States in Malaysia	*Number of Pre-War Buildings*	*Percentage (%)*
Penang	5057	24.3
Perak	3351	16.1
Johor	2323	11.2
Malacca	2177	10.5
Koala Lumpur	1763	8.4

The management of culture and heritage in Malaysia was put under the Ministry of Tourism and Culture, established on the 20th of May 1987, combining Department of Culture from the Ministry of Culture, Youths and Sports with the Malaysian Tourism Development Corporation from the Ministry of Trade and Industries. On 22nd October 1992, the ministry was renamed into Ministry of Culture, Arts and Tourism.

This ministry was later divided in Mac 2004, into two ministries, namely the Tourism Ministry and Ministry of Culture, Arts and Heritage. This separation is seen as recognition of tourism as a potential number one sector of the country and a move to appreciate the value of heritage of the country.

Agencies under this ministry are the National Archives, the National Art and Gallery, the Department of Museum and Antiquities, Malaysian Handicrafts (Kraftangan Malaysia), the National Film Development Corporation (Finas), the National Art Academy, the National Library and the Istana Budaya (the Culture

Palace). Despite the move to strengthen the ministries, the separation of the cultural elements from the Tourism Ministry can give impacts on the direction of 'cultural and heritage tourism', leaving this niche area as an no-man's land!

The Formulation of National Cultural Policy

At a national conference organized by Malaysia's Ministry of Culture, Youth and Sports in 1971, the Malaysian government formulated what was to become a national cultural policy based on the following principles:

(i) The national culture of Malaysia must henceforth be based on the cultures of the people indigenous to the region.

(ii) Elements from other cultures which are judged suitable and reasonable may be incorporated into Malaysia's national culture.

(iii) Islam will be an important element in the national culture.

In the period since its implementation, Malaysia's national culture policy has become one important point of vigorous debate and political conflict. In the years since the formulation of a National Cultural Policy, and particularly in the late 1980's, the Malaysian government has been concerned to implement its basic principles by intervening directly and across the board in the cultural field. Not surprisingly, and perhaps because it has not been altogether clear and efficient about its task, government intervention in the cultural field has produced a response on the part of a variety of non-Malaya groups who feel that their cultural freedom has been curtailed.

For example, at a meeting of the Chinese guild and associations of Malaysia held in March, 1983, delegates passed a series of resolutions that were compiled in a joint memorandum to the Ministry of Culture, Youth and Sports.

In April 1984, a group of the best-known Indian cultural, social and religious organizations submitted a similar memorandum. Both memoranda accused the government of having formulated a cultural policy which was Malaya-centric and undemocratic, and requested that a new policy on national culture be established which was more clearly multi-ethnic and democratic.

Law and Legislations on Cultural and Heritage Properties

The legal foundations of the Malaysian cultural policy are derived from the following acts and regulations:

i) Antiquities Act 1976 (Act 168).

ii) National Art Gallery Act, 1958.

iii) Legal Deposit of Library Material Act, 1986 (Act A667).

iv) National Library Act, 1972; The National Library (Amendment) Act, 1987.

v) National Archive Act, 1966 (Act 44), (Revised 1971), (Act A85), (Revised 1993), (Act 511).

vi) Tourist Development Corporation of Malaysia Act 1972 (Act 1972).

vii) Broadcasting Act 1988 (Act 338), Broadcasting (Amendment) Act, 1997 (Act A977).

viii) Cinematography Film-Hire Duty Act 1965 (Revised 1990), (Act 434).

ix) (Perbadanan Kemajuan File Nasional Malaysia Act 1981 (Act 244), Perbadanan Kemajuan File Nasional Malaysia (Amendment) Act, 1984 (Act 589).

x) Perbadanan Kemajuan Kraftangan Malaysia Act 1979 (Act 222).

xi) Theatres & Places of Public Amusement (Federal Territory) Act 1988 (Act 182).

xii) Bernama Act, 1967 (Revised 1990), (Act 449).

xiii) Entertainment Duty Act 1953 (Revised 1973) (Act 103).

Efforts to preserve the heritage buildings in Malaysia are supported by various acts and legislations. The prominent acts have been the Town and Country Planning Act of 1976 or the 172 Act, The National Land Code (Kanun Tanah Negara), the Street, Drainage and Building Act 133, the Antiquities Act 1976, as well as local legislations such as the Malacca Enactment No. 6 (1988).

Act 133 for instance stipulates that "No person shall erect any building without a prior written permission of the local authority".

This provision is supported by Section 18 of Act 172 which states "All land/building use shall comply with the local plans (structure and local plans). Any development shall obtain planning permission. And if there is no development plan prepared for the area, the owner/developer of the land shall inform their plan to the adjoining landowners (Act 172,).

To date, a guidelines on the Guidelines on the Conservation of George Town Inner City details out specific recommendations pertaining extensions, renovations, revitalizations of heritage buildings within the prescribed zones.

At present, any erection of buildings is loosely bonded by both Acts (133 and 172). Section 16 of 133 defines erections of building includes 'renews or repairs of any existing buildings in such a manner as to involve a renewal, reconstruction or erection of any portion of an outer or party wall to the extent of one storey height". Further, all building that fall within the definition of development, stipulated in Act 172 also requires planning permission. The Guidelines is in concordant with Part Vll of Act 133 that gives the State Authority to make bylaws or in respect of every purpose which is deemed by him necessary. In regards to the preservation of buildings, the State Authority, among other things, has the right to make by laws in:-

(i) The construction, paving, width and level of arcades and footways;

(ii) The construction, alteration and demolition of buildings and the methods and materials to be used in connection therewith;

(iii) The minimum timber or other building material content in any building.

Issues

The promotion of culture and heritage in Malaysia faces several underlying issues that both are related to the complexity of the society living in Malaysia. Among the issues are:-

8

Economic and Financial Development of Tourism

Time is a valuable commodity for today's travellers. Dual-income families find it difficult to schedule vacation time; family members often have jobs or activities that conflict; or an individual's job makes long vacations impractical. As a result, more families and individuals are taking long weekend or holiday vacations, or extending business trips into short getaway vacations. Packaging is a popular technique used for attracting these customers, because packages make travel easier and more convenient.

In the hospitality and tourism industry, "packaging" is the process of combining two or more related and complementary offerings into a single-price offering. A package may include a wide variety of services such as lodging, meals, entrance fees to attractions, entertainment, transportation costs (air, auto, train, cab or bus), guide services, or other similar activities. Packaging can also create a variety of benefits for participating businesses. This publication will: Identify reasons for the increased popularity of packaging. Address issues a business should consider when developing a package. Describe the components of successful packages. Discuss the process of pricing a package.

Why Packages are Popular

Travel packages have become increasingly popular over the years. They are attractive because they benefit both the customer and participating businesses; packaging provides convenience and value to the customer, and added revenue for participating businesses.

Items to Consider in Developing a Package

Before developing a tourism packaging program, the business should devise a marketing plan through practical marketing research. The business owner should ask him/herself the following questions: Are you willing to do market research to determine who your customers are and what they want? What are the potential attractions, businesses, or marketing service firms that could provide a part of the package? Meet with the managers of these businesses and public attractions to discuss their interests and ideas. What are potential marketing and promotional networks that will help spread the word about your product?

Convention and visitors bureaus, chambers of commerce, retail travel agents, clubs and organizations, state offices of tourism, and other attractions or travel businesses all have the potential to play an important role in merchandising your package. Will the physical appearance and service skills of your business match the target audience? Does your business have the ability to manage and service the customers you generate through your packaging program? Are you prepared for a risk? Because you will be including customer service activities that are not under your direct control, you will be required to develop formal, written agreements between the cooperating businesses.

Benefits to the Customer

Packaging can be an effective marketing tool to provide several customer benefits. These may include: Ability to budget for trips. Packages include most of the components a customer must pay for during a trip. The customer pays at one time and has a good idea of the trip's total cost. Increased convenience. Trips can be time consuming and difficult to arrange. Several telephone calls and letters may be required to arrange for tickets, accommodations, reservations, and other components of a trip. A package allows a customer to arrange many components of a trip with one call or letter and one payment, saving the customer time and aggravation.

Greater economy. Businesses that package can frequently purchase tickets, meals, and other package components at wholesale prices. The business can add in the cost of packaging and still provide a competitive price to the customer. Thus, the cost to the customer is usually more economical than purchasing the package components individually. Popular programs and activities. Visitors and travellers are often unfamiliar with many of the activities and attractions in an area: a package can help customers find them easily.

Specialized interests. Packaging provides a unique opportunity to design components of a package for specialized interests. These so-called "benefit bundles" can include a package component not readily available to individual customers. For example, a package weekend may feature a cooking demonstration by a well-known chef or a lecture by a well-known author. Benefits to Participating Businesses Packaging can be used by businesses to help improve profitability and build customer volume. Examples include:

Improved profitability. During peak or high-demand periods, use packaging to add value to an existing product. Purchasers may be required to stay a prescribed period or purchase a combination of goods and services. Packaging may also allow a business to price its product at a premium by adding special goods and services. Smooth business patterns. Use packaging during low demand periods to add attractive features to the business's service or product, thus generating additional business. Other businesses may also be willing, to discount their services during this time. Adding these services to the existing product mix may generate new business.

Joint marketing opportunities. Packaging can allow the business to reduce marketing costs or start a new program one could not normally afford by joining with one or more businesses to conduct a marketing or advertising program. This strategy can be especially effective if the businesses involved have similar customers. Improved target marketing. Packaging can be an effective tool to tailor tourism and travel products for specific target markets. Examples can be ski, sports, or theatre weekends. Good market research is needed so an appropriate mix of tourism and travel services will meet the needs and desires of a target group of customers. Greater holiday weekend business. Packaging can be used to highlight special holiday weekends by developing services appropriate to the theme of the weekend. New Year's, Valentine's Day, or Mother's Day are just a few of the holidays that can be used to develop special programs for parties, couples, or family gifts. Unique recurring events. Businesses can create their own events that can occur throughout the year. Events could be tournaments such as chess or bridge or crime re-enactments that let guests do the detective work. Events of this type will require imagination and inventiveness to take advantage of the wide variety of activities that take place in the community. This technique is often called "programming."

Redirected traffic to lesser-known attractions. Directing visitors to often overlooked attractions can help in two ways: heavily visited attractions may be offered some relief, while newly discovered attractions may thrive and prosper. Businesses can use many different strategies in designing a package product. Success will depend on good market research, an understanding of existing customers, research, an understanding of existing customers, and a good knowledge of the community and its activities.

Pricing a Package

Lodging or transportation—the most expensive parts of a package product-are usually the first contact points for customers who purchase a packaged vacation or travel product. Lodging operations or travel agents are usually the key to organizing a packaging program, even though an area's attractions may bring visitors to a community. Although accommodations and transportation are the basic ingredients of a package, tickets to attractions, dining, and other services are other key parts of the product mix that make the package marketable. It is necessary for a business to understand its target market and conduct basic practical market research in order to develop a successful package. Experimenting with a set of packages can also help you identify which sets of activities are most attractive to your customers.

Issues to consider when pricing a package include: The package must be a good value and competitive in the market. Customers should not be able to purchase separate items in the package for less than the package price. A large user of package components should be able to receive discounts from businesses that provide them. Evaluate the role packaging can play in the business's marketing program. While packaging can be used to implement many different strategies, the basic intent is to generate additional business. Determine if the package is feasible by applying a break-even analysis to help determine how many packages a business must sell before earning a profit.

Break-Even Analysis

Break-even analysis is a tool used to determine total sales needed to recoup costs, hence the name "break-even." This analysis technique can also be used to evaluate alternative pricing levels.

Elements of a Successful Package

Putting together a successful package is not easy. However, by following the suggestions listed below, the chances of success will be greater. Include attractions or demand generators. Every package needs one or more core attractions. These could be tickets to a special event, specialized programming, or reduced prices. Provide value to the customer. Many travellers buy packages because they perceive they will receive greater value for the travel dollars they spend. For some, this translates into a package that costs less than the sum of the regular prices of individual elements. Almost everybody is interested in getting something for nothing or next to nothing. Be well planned and coordinated. A successful package must be well planned and coordinated. Each element should flow naturally from one to the next. Use a theme to hold the package together and create a positive experience for the tourist.

Offer consistent quality and compatibility among elements. Many customers buy packages because they expect consistency in quality. Combine only package components that are compatible and enhance the overall quality of the traveller's experience. Customer dissatisfaction with one part of the package will often spoil the entire experience. Provide a distinctive customer benefit. The best packages provide customers something they would not get if they purchased package elements separately. Sometimes this benefit is the offer of value, but in other cases, it is a component that is not readily available to individual customers.

This might involve incorporating special lectures or appearances, unique dining experiences, or other activities. Cover all the details. The temptation might be to throw a package together, but the close attention to detail makes some packages more successful than others. Remember, it is often the little things a business does for guests that matter the most. Some things to consider include a policy on refunds and cancellations and complete information on all package elements included in the price, as well as items not included. Generate a profit. Clearly, packages offer a unique way to satisfy traveller needs and wants. Of course, the package should also be designed to generate a profit. The ideal time to offer packages is when demand is low and when the package will not displace customers who may generate higher revenues.

Tourism Contribution to Economic Conservation

The main positive economic impacts of tourism relate to foreign exchange earnings, contributions to government revenues, and generation of employment and business opportunities. These are discussed briefly here; further information on economic contributions from tourism can be found at the World Travel & Tourism Council's home page.

Foreign Exchange Earnings

Tourism expenditures and the export and import of related goods and services generate income to the host economy and can stimulate the investment necessary to finance growth in other economic sectors. Some countries seek to accelerate this growth by requiring visitors to bring in a certain amount of foreign currency for each day of their stay and do not allow them to take it out of the country again at the end of the trip.

An important indicator of the role of international tourism is its generation of foreign exchange earnings. Tourism is one of the top five export categories for as many as 83% of countries and is a main source of foreign exchange earnings for at least 38% of countries.

Contribution to Government Revenues

Government revenues from the tourism sector can be categorized as direct and indirect contributions. Direct contributions are generated by taxes on incomes from tourism employment and tourism businesses, and by direct levies on tourists such as departure taxes. Indirect contributions are those originated from taxes and duties levied on goods and services supplied to tourists.

The United States National Park Service estimates that the 273 million visits to American national parks in 1993 generated direct and indirect expenditures of US$ 10 billion and 200,000 jobs. When visits to land managed by other agencies, and to state, local, and privately-managed parks, are added, parks were estimated to bring around US$ 22 billion annually to the US economy. These expenditures also generate significant tax revenues for the government. The World Travel and Tourism Council estimates that travel and tourism's direct, indirect, and personal tax contribution worldwide was over US$ 800 billion in 1998-a.

Employment Generation

The rapid expansion of international tourism has led to significant employment creation. For example, the hotel accommodation sector alone provided around 11.3 million jobs worldwide in 1995. Tourism can generate jobs directly through hotels, restaurants, nightclubs, taxis, and souvenir sales, and indirectly through the supply of goods and services needed by tourism-related businesses. According to the WTO, tourism supports some 7% of the world's workers.

Stimulation of Infrastructure Investment

Tourism can induce the local government to make infrastructure improvements such as better water and sewage systems, roads, electricity, telephone and public transport networks, all of which can improve the quality of life for residents as well as facilitate tourism.

Contribution to Local Economies

Tourism can be a significant, even essential, part of the local economy. As the environment is a basic component of the tourism industry's assets, tourism revenues are often used to measure the economic value of protected areas.

For example, Dorrigo National Park in New South Wales, Australia, has been estimated to contribute 7% of gross regional output and 8.4% of regional employment. The importance of tourism to local economies can also be illustrated by the impacts when it is disrupted: the catastrophic 1997 floods that closed Yosemite National Park in California cause locally severe economic losses to the areas around the park. In the most heavily impacted county, Mariposa County, 1997 personal income was reduced by an estimated US$1,159 per capita (US$18 million for the entire county)-a 6.6% decline. The county was also estimated to have lost US$1.67 million in county occupancy and sales tax revenues, and 956 jobs, a significant number in a county of fewer than 16,000 residents.

There are other local revenues that are not easily quantified, as not all tourist expenditures are formally registered in the macroeconomic statistics. Money is earned from tourism through informal employment such as street vendors, informal guides, rickshaw drivers, etc. The positive side of informal or unreported employment is that the money is returned to the local economy, and has a great multiplier effect as it is spent over and over again. The World Travel and Tourism Council estimates that tourism generates an indirect contribution equal to 100% of direct tourism expenditures.

The Economic Impacts of Ecotourism

There are two related, but distinct, economic concepts in Ecotourism: economic impact and economic value. This issues paper focusses on economic impact, which refers to the change in sales, income, jobs, or other parameter generated by Ecotourism. A common Ecotourism goal is the generation of economic benefits, whether they be profits for companies, jobs for communities, or revenues for parks. Ecotourism plays a particularly important role because it can create jobs in remote regions that historically have benefited less from economic development programs than have more populous areas. Even a small number of jobs may be significant in communities where populations are low and alternatives are few. This economic impact can increase political and financial support for conservation.

Protected areas, and nature conservation generally, provide many benefits to society, including preservation of biodiversity, maintenance of watersheds, and so on. Unfortunately, many of these benefits are intangible. However, the benefits associated with recreation and tourism in protected areas tend to be tangible. For example, divers at a marine park spend money on lodging, food, and other goods and services, thereby providing employment for local and nonlocal residents. These positive economic impacts can lead to increased support for the protected areas with which they are associated. This is one reason why Ecotourism has been embraced as a means for enhancing conservation of natural resources. Several studies in Australia and elsewhere have assessed the economic impacts of Ecotourism.

Predictably, the level of benefits varies widely as a result of differences in the quality of the attraction, access, and so on. In some cases, the number of jobs created will be low, but in rural areas even a few jobs can make a big difference. Still, Ecotourism benefits should not be oversold, or there may be a backlash as reality fails to live up to expectations. The impacts of Ecotourism, or any economic activity, can be grouped into three categories: direct, indirect, and induced. Direct impacts are those arising from the initial tourism spending, such as money spent at a restaurant. The restaurant buys goods and services (inputs) from other businesses, thereby generating indirect impacts. In addition, the restaurant employees spend part of their wages to buy various goods and services, thereby generating induced impacts. Of course, if the restaurant purchases the goods and services from outside the region of interest, then the money provides no indirect impact to the region — it leaks away. By identifying the leakages, or conversely the linkages within the economy, the indirect and induced impacts of tourism can be estimated.

In addition, this information can be used to identify what goods are needed but are not being produced in the region, how much demand there is for such goods, and what the likely benefits of local production would be. This enables policy makers to determine priorities for developing inputs for use by the tourism or other industries. How, then, are these direct, indirect, and induced impacts to be estimated? For small areas with non-diverse economies, there are relatively few indirect and induced impacts, and there are relatively little data available for modelling these impacts. Therefore, surveys of visitors, residents, and/or businesses often are used to identify tourism's direct impacts. For larger areas, such as states or countries, economists have developed various techniques for estimating indirect and induced impacts, including computable general equilibrium (CGE) and input-output (IO) analysis.

Negative Economic Impacts of Tourism

There are many hidden costs to tourism, which can have unfavourable economic effects on the host community. Often rich countries are better able to profit from tourism than poor ones. Whereas the least developed countries have the most urgent need for income, employment and general rise of the standard of living by means of tourism, they are least able to realize these benefits. Among the reasons for this are large-scale transfer of tourism revenues out of the host country and exclusion of local businesses and products.

Leakage

The direct income for an area is the amount of tourist expenditure that remains locally after taxes, profits, and wages are paid outside the area and after imports are purchased; these subtracted amounts are called leakage. In most all-inclusive package tours, about 80% of travellers' expenditures go to the airlines, hotels and other international companies (who often have their headquarters in the travellers' home countries), and not to local businesses or workers. In addition, significant amounts of income actually retained at destination level can leave again through leakage. A study of tourism 'leakage' in Thailand estimated that 70% of all money spent by tourists ended up leaving Thailand (via foreign-owned tour operators, airlines, hotels, imported drinks and food, etc.). Estimates for other Third World countries range from 80% in the Caribbean to 40% in India.

Source: Sustainable Living

Of each US$ 100 spent on a vacation tour by a tourist from a developed country, only around US$ 5 actually stays in a developing-country destination's economy.

There are two main ways that leakage occurs: Import Leakage: This commonly occurs when tourists demand standards of equipment, food, and other products that the host country cannot supply. Especially in less-developed countries, food and drinks must often be imported, since local products are not up to the hotel's (i.e. tourist's) standards or the country simply doesn't have a supplying industry. Much of the income from tourism expenditures leaves the country again to pay for these imports.

The average import-related leakage for most developing countries today is between 40% and 50% of gross tourism earnings for small economies and between 10% and 20% for most advanced and diversified economies, according to UNCTAD. Even in developed regions, local producers are often unable to supply the tourism industry appropriately even if good will is present: the 64-room hotel "Kaiser im Tyrol" in Austria, an award-winning leader in sustainable practices, cannot find organic food suppliers in the local farming networks in the appropriate quantity, quality and reliability, as production cycles and processes are not compatible with its needs.

Source: Austrian Preparatory Conference for the International Year of Ecotourism, September 2001 Export leakage Multinational corporations and large foreign businesses have a substantial share in the import leakage. Often, especially in poor developing destinations, they are the only ones that possess the necessary capital to invest in the construction of tourism infrastructure and facilities. As a consequence of this, an export leakage arises when overseas investors who finance the resorts and hotels take their profits back to their country of origin.

A 1996 UN report evaluating the contribution of tourism to national income, gross levels of incomes or gross foreign exchange, found that net earnings of tourism, after deductions were made for all necessary foreign exchange expenditures, were much more significant for the industry. This report found significant leakage associated with: (a) imports of materials and equipment for construction; (b) imports of consumer goods, particularly food and drinks; (c) repatriation of profits earned by foreign investors; (d) overseas promotional expenditures and (e) amortization of external debt incurred in the development of hotels and resorts.

The impact of the leakage varied greatly across countries, depending on the structure of the economy and the tourism industry. From the data presented in this study on the Caribbean, St. Lucia had a foreign exchange leakage rate of 56% from its gross tourism receipts, Aruba had 41%, Antigua and Barbuda 25% and Jamaica 40%.

Source: Caribbean Voice

Enclave Tourism: Local businesses often see their chances to earn income from tourists severely reduced by the creation of "all-inclusive" vacation packages. When tourists remain for their entire stay at the same cruise ship or resort, which provides everything they need and where they will make all their expenditures, not much opportunity is left for local people to profit from tourism.

The Organization of American States (OAS) carried out a survey of Jamaica's tourist industry that looked at the role of the all-inclusives compared to other types of accommodation. It found that 'All-inclusive hotels generate the largest amount of revenue but their impact on the economy is smaller per dollar of revenue than other accommodation subsectors.'

It also concluded that all-inclusives imported more, and employed fewer people per dollar of revenue than other hotels. This information confirms the concern of those who have argued that all-inclusives have a smaller trickle-down effect on local economies.

The cruise ship industry provides another example of economic enclave tourism. Non-river cruises carried some 8.7 million international passengers in 1999. On many ships, especially in the Caribbean (the world's most popular cruise destination with 44.5% of cruise passengers), guests are encouraged to spend most of their time and money on board, and opportunities to spend in some ports are closely managed and restricted.

Bibliography

Bhushan Ekta : *Developing Professionalism in Hospitality : Aviation Sector,*, Rajat Publications, Delhi, 2010.

Brunt, Paul: *Market Research in Travel and Tourism,* Oxford, Butterworth Heinemann, 1997.

Coccosis, Harry and Nijkamp, Peter: *Sustainable Tourism Development,* Aldershot, Avebury, 1995.

Cournoyer, Norman G.: *Hotel, Restaurant, and Travel Law: A Preventive Approach,* Albany, Delmar Publishers, 1993.

Davidoff, Donald M.: *Customer Service in the Hospitality and Tourism Industry,* Englewood Cliffs, Prentice Hall, 1994.

Dayal Shambhu : *Ethical Foundation of Hotel and Hospitality Managemen,* Akansha, Delhi, 2006.

Eberts, Marjorie: *Careers in Travel, Tourism, and Hospitality,* Lincolnwood, VGM Career Horizons, 1997.

Fowler, Peter: *Heritage and Tourism: In the Global Village,* London, Retailed, 1993.

Frechtling, Douglas C: *Practical Tourism Forecasting,* Oxford, Butterworth Heinemann, 1996.

Gunn, Clare and Var, Turgut: *Tourism Planning,* London, Retailed, 2002.

Hays, Judi Radice: *Restaurant & Food Graphics,* Glen Cove, PBC International, 1994.

Horner, S. and Swarbrooke, J.: *Marketing Tourism, Hospitality and Leisure in Europe,* London, International Thomson Business Press, 1996.

Jack, G and Phipps, A: *Tourism and Intercultural Exchange: Why Tourism Matters,* Clevedon, Channel View, 2005.

Jakle, John: *Tourist, The: Travel in Twentieth Century North America,* University of North Nebraska, 1985.

Jennings, Gayle: *Tourism Research,* Chichester, Wiley, 2001.

Judd, D R: *Promoting Tourism* in US Cities, 1995.

Karski, A: *Urban Tourism* - A Key to Urban Regeneration?, 1990.

Kharbanda, O. and E. Stallworthy: *Waste Management Towards a Sustainable Society,* Auburn House, New York, 1990.

Kotler, Philip et al: *Marketing Places: Attracting Investment, Industry & Tourism etc,* New York, free press, 1993.

Labarge, Margaret Wade: *Medieval Travellers: The Rich and Restless,* London, Hamish Hamilton, 1982.

Larkham, P J: *Building a New Heritage: Tourism, Culture & Identity in the New Europe,* London, Routledge,1994.

Lawrence, E. : *Technology of internet business,* Wiley, Australia, 2002.

Laws, Eric: *Tourist Destination Management: Issues, Analysis & Policies,* London, Routledge, 1995.

Leed, Eric J: *Mind of the Traveller, The: From Gilgamesh to Global Tourism,* New York, 1991.

Leivadi, S: *Sociology of Tourism, The: Theoretical And Empirical Investigations,* London, Retailed, 1996.

Lucas, Rosemary E.: *Managing Employee Relations in the Hotel and Catering Industry,* London, Cassell, 1995.

Marcussen, Carl H. : *Internet Distribution of European Travel and Tourism Services,* Research Centre of Bornholm, Denmark, 1999.

Pant Anoop : *Accountancy for the Hospitality Industry,* Rajat Pub, Delhi, 2008.

Peters, M: *International Tourism,* London, Hutchinson, 1969.

Prentice, R: *Conceptualising The Experiences of Heritage Tourists,* 1997.

Robinson, M, Evans, E & Chalazion, P: *Tourism and Cultural Change, Sunderland,* Business Education Publishers Ltd, 1996.

Rogers, H Anthea and Slinn, Judy A: *Tourism: Management of Facilities,* London, Pitman: M & E, 1993.

Schwaninger, M: *Trends in Leisure and Tourism for 2000 - 2010,* Prentice Hall, 1989.

Scottish Tourist Board: *Visitor Attractions: A Development Guide,* Edinburgh, Scottish Tourist Board, 1991.

Seaton, A V et al: *Tourism: The state of the Art,* Chichester, John Wiley, 1994.

Sharma Jitendra K. *: Contemporary Tourism and Hospitality Management,* Kanishka, Delhi, 2006.

Shaw, G and Williams, A: *Tourism and Tourism Spaces,* London, Sage, 2004.

Sheldon, P. : *Tourism Information Technology,* CABI Publishing, Oxford, England, 1997.

Wahab, S A: *Tourism Management,* Tourism International Press, 1975.

Werthner, H. and Klein, S. : *Information Technology and Tourism-A challenging relationship,* Springer, New York, 1999.

Index

❑❑❑